ANTLERS:
NATURE'S MAJESTIC CROWN

A SPECTACULAR TRIBUTE TO THE ANTLERED ANIMALS
OF NORTH AMERICA AND EUROPE

TEXT BY ERWIN A. BAUER
PHOTOGRAPHS BY ERWIN AND PEGGY BAUER

VOYAGEUR PRESS

Edited by Mary Katherine Parks and Helene Anderson
Designed by Lou Gordon and Kathryn Mallien
Printed in China
95 96 97 98 99   5 4 3 2 1

Library of Congress Cataloging-in-Publication Data
Antlers : nature's majestic crown / by Erwin A. Bauer, Peggy Bauer.
p.   cm.
Includes bibliographical references (p. 155) and index.
ISBN 0-89658-253-1
1. Antlers. 2. Cervidae. I. Bauer, Peggy. II. Title.
QL942.B36   1995
599.73'5704471—dc20   94-9033
CIP

Published by Voyageur Press, Inc.
P.O. Box 338, 123 North Second Street, Stillwater, MN 55082 U.S.A.
612-430-2210, fax 612-430-2211

Distributed in Canada by Raincoast Books, 112 East Third Avenue, Vancouver, B.C. V5T 1C8

Please write or call, or stop by, for our free catalog of natural history publications. Our toll-free
number to place an order or to obtain a free catalog is 800-888-WOLF (800-888-9653).

Educators, fundraisers, premium and gift buyers, publicists, and marketing managers: Looking for
creative products and new sales ideas? Voyageur Press books are available at special discounts
when purchased in quantities, and special editions can be created to your specifications. For details
contact our marketing department.

The whitetail in the background would qualify for listing in the Boone and Crockett record book. The foreground deer is exceptional as well.

DEDICATIONS

To the many organizations that are dedicated to wildlife conservation and to saving forever the habitat of the animals in this book:

> Foundation for North American Big Game, Greater Yellowstone Coalition, Boone and Crockett Club, Canadian Nature Federation, Defenders of Wildlife, Montana Wilderness Association, National Audubon Society, National Wildlife Federation, National Parks and Conservation Association, Nature Conservancy, Pope and Young Club, Rocky Mountain Elk Foundation, Sierra Club, Whitetails Forever, Wilderness Society, Wildlife Conservation Society, and the World Wildlife Fund.

This book is also dedicated to the following friends of antlered animals:

> Brent and Robin Allen, Charles Alsheimer, Hefner Appling, Dick Buchonis, Murry Burnham, Jay Diest, Fossil Rim Wildlife Center, Gill Gigstead, Allen and Larry Grimland of the Whitetail Ranch, Bob and Judy Hoy, George T. Jambers Jr., Clarence Johnstone, Kermit Klaerner, Mike Loss, Malcolm Mackenzie, Northwest Trek, Dan and Uli Nowlan, Gap and Peggy Puchi, Roy Randall, Bob Reagan, Frank and Homer Sayers, and George Smith.

CONTENTS

❧❧

An Alaskan Barren Ground caribou bull in Denali National Park.

INTRODUCTION

In a run-down section of central San Antonio, Texas, is a shrine that some consider as hallowed as the Alamo. It is the Buckhorn Hall of Horns, located in the Lone Star Brewery, where one of the world's largest collections of whitetailed deer heads stares silently from dusty walls. One of these heads, long a world's record, has an incredible seventy-eight points. Thousands make a pilgrimage here every year from far beyond Texas just to see these antlers. And to dream.

Many more marvel at another extraordinary antler and horn display, the Boone and Crockett Club's National Collection, which hangs on the log walls of a hunting cabin in the Buffalo Bill Historical Center in Cody, Wyoming. This shrine contains some of the largest known antlers of several species of North American deer, including world's record woodland, Barren Ground, and Quebec-Labrador caribou, and Sitka blacktailed deer, among many other near world's records.

Halfway around the world, in the cavernous ballroom of an old hunting lodge near Braemar, Scotland, is a great antler canopy that makes the Buckhorn and Buffalo Bill bragging collections seem almost humble. Here are the mounted heads or skulls of more than three thousand red deer stags taken on the seventy-seven-thousand-acre (30,800-hectare) estate that once belonged to Queen Victoria's granddaughter. The caretaker claims it is the granddaddy of all antler collections, and it just may be.

There is a great variety of antler conformations. This Minnesota whitetail buck has "high" antlers, somewhat unusual in that state.

A whitetail's antlers can take on strange, even bizarre conformations due to heredity, injury, disease, insect infestation, or some other cause. These are unusual examples from Buckhorn Hall of Horns in San Antonio, Texas.

Antlers. Since the dawn of history humans have been fascinated by them. Some fifteen thousand years ago, a Stone Age man crouched in a cave in southern France and, by flickering torch light, applied oxide pigments to a limestone wall. His accurate depiction of a red deer stag (and other creatures) still can be seen in these now famous caverns of Lascaux. Elsewhere in deep canyons and hidden grottoes all across the northern hemisphere are other, lesser known pictographs and rock paintings of animals with antlers. In many, the ancient artists drew the antlers larger than they actually could have been, just as today's trophy collectors exaggerate antler size.

Once during a whitewater trip down Idaho's "River of No Return," the turbulent Middle Fork of the Salmon, we beached our raft long enough to stretch our legs. From streamside, we followed a faint game trail far into a deep ravine that no other people had recently explored. Sitting down to rest, someone spotted an old and badly faded sketch in red paint of either an elk or a mule deer with long, backward curving antlers. Who knows how long ago that Native American artist-hunter had walked away from here, carrying his trophy?

Later on that same trip we pitched our overnight camp on a river sandbar crisscrossed by deer tracks. Into a fallen tree trunk nearby, a latter-day deer hunter had carved this message with his hunting knife: "R. Miller shot his biggest buck here on Oct 24, 71." Probably R. Miller, like many other outdoors enthusiasts across the United States and Canada, is best known in his community, his club, and his workplace for his skill as a hunter. Or more likely by the dimensions of the antlers hanging on his wall.

FROM DINNER TABLE
TO MEDICINE CABINET

Primitive peoples made some of their first tools, weapons, and ornaments from cast (dropped or shed) antlers. And craftspeople still do so today, using the tough material to produce everything from handsome knife handles and belt buckles, to buttons, pipes, ladles, cribbage boards, and jewelry. For centuries in Asia, ground-up antlers have been prescribed for everything from acid stomach and baldness to arthritis, rheumatism, impotence, and forgetfulness. Though there is little evidence that the medicine is helpful—except psychologically—the demand for antlers as a

THE COST OF THE DREAM

Trophy antlers have at times been more valuable than gold. Probably the most expensive rack in history belonged to the Moritzburg sixty-six-point stag (which actually had only sixty-two points), shot in 1696 by King Frederick I of Prussia. According to legend, it was driven toward the king's stand by the gamekeeper's daughter riding on a tame elk (known as "moose" in North America). Later the king traded the antlers to Frederick Augustus of Saxony for an entire company—two hundred—of the tallest grenadier guards in his realm. Augustus wanted the head for his vast antler collection at Schloss (Castle) Moritzburg near Dresden, Germany, where it still collects dust.

For countless hunters worldwide, the pursuit of trophy antlers borders on being a religious experience. In 1991 in just one U.S. state, Texas, 600,000 licensed hunters spent over five million days and over a billion dollars to obtain the antlers of what they regard as the greatest game animal on earth, the whitetailed deer.

pharmaceutical is great enough to support a worldwide industry of deer farms and ranches. And, unfortunately, poaching.

To help supply the demand for antlers, an unusual event is held each spring in northwest Wyoming. It is the Jackson Hole Antler Roundup. For a week or so, troops of Boy Scouts scour the nearby National Elk Refuge, where about ten thousand elk spend the bitter winter, to collect several tons of antlers dropped by the bulls shortly before they return to their summer range. These antlers are then sold at auction to buyers from Korea and Taiwan. Enough profit is made annually to support the elk winter-feeding program, as well as many Boy Scout conservation activities.

Antlers have served as a symbol of strength and health, of rank, power or prestige, as well as of wildness. Antlers appear on royal coats of arms and on the postage stamps of many lands. Roman legions marched across Europe behind a golden eagle perched on the antler of a mighty stag. Antlers hang in rude trappers' camps beside Louisiana bayous, over fire-

Facing page: *A handsome mule deer with large antler rack in winter.* **Above:** *A fine specimen of a North American bull elk with large antlers—a near record-book-size pair.*

places in log hunting cabins in Manitoba, in air-conditioned corporate offices in Los Angeles, and in stone castles from Sweden to Spain. To own a massive, or better still, the *most* massive set of antlers from any kind of deer assures the owner high status no matter where he or she lives.

Large handsome antlers have also worked their magic on me. I admire those impressive heads hanging on walls, but I am much more fascinated with those on the hoof—those still carried intact by their original live owners. Hunting these splendid ruminants, at first with a gun and during the past quarter-century with only a camera, has taken me to some of the most wild, most haunting, lonely, and beautiful places left in the world.

I think especially of one November dusk. All day long the weather had been foul, and snow swirled over the Absaroka–Beartooth Wilderness Area, near where Peggy and I live in Paradise Valley, Montana. Heading homeward with camera and lenses in a backpack, I began to hike faster and faster to stay warm. Suddenly, in a final, completely unexpected shaft of sunlight, I saw the pearl-tipped antlers of a fine bull elk illuminated against an ominous blue-black sky ahead of me. I fumbled in the backpack to retrieve the camera, but I wasn't fast enough. Nevertheless that eerie scene is a "trophy" I'll carry with me forever.

So is another, very similar moment, this one during the 1960s on the opposite side of the globe in Iran, before turmoil and revolution consumed that land. Near dusk of a gloomy day I sat, weary and footsore, on a ridge of the Elburz Mountains in (then) Mohammad Reza Shah National Park, watching another ridge where a herd of bachelor red deer grazed unaware. Then for a minute at most, the last ray of a golden setting sun focused directly on the antlers like a benediction, and seemed to set them on fire. Then night fell. I sat in darkness for a long while before rising to trudge toward camp.

That's what I mean about antlers being mystical.

Antlers have served as a symbol of strength and health, of rank, power, or prestige, as well as of wildness. **Inset:** *The world's largest concentration of elk, and the best place to view them in winter, close up, is the National Elk Refuge at Jackson, Wyoming, where thousands are fed by humans every year. Later, the antlers discarded on the refuge are collected by Boy Scouts and sold at auction in Jackson to support conservation activities.*

ANTLERS

Biologists generally agree that forty different species and about five times that many races or subspecies of deer inhabit the earth. Together they comprise the family Cervidae.

Fortunately, five of the forty species — the mule deer, whitetailed deer, moose, elk, and caribou native to North America — are relatively easy to find, some being as handy as our suburban flower gardens and public parks. Most of those in Europe are also easy to see. To view the rest would require slogging through swamps and rainforests, scaling mountain ranges, hiking among silent evergreens, wandering over bleak tundra, and crossing hot, dry plains on every continent except Antarctica. Not easy work, it's true, but certainly high adventure. And the searcher would eventually meet some of the handsomest, swiftest, most elusive and interesting members of the animal kingdom. They go by such romantic, strange sounding names as barasinga and brocket, maral and muntjac, chital, huemul, and pudu, Pere David's, Thorold's, and hog deer.

What sets all of these deer apart from other living things is that the male Cervidae grow and discard antlers every year. No other animals do this, except for the very small Chinese water deer and the musk deer of eastern Asia that grow tusks instead of antlers. Caribou and reindeer females *do* grow antlers, but these average much smaller than those of males.

❧ ❧

A bull elk stands in a Yellowstone National Park meadow near the end of August. The velvet is peeling from its antlers; soon the rut will begin. The bull is sleek and fat, but it will lose some of this weight by not feeding during the breeding season. Three weeks after this photo was taken the antlers were bare and polished, and the animal had acquired a harem of cows.

CLASSIFICATION OF THE DEER OF NORTH AMERICA AND EUROPE

Family	Subfamily	Genus	Species	Common name
Cervidae	Alcinae	Alces	Alces alces	moose, European elk
	Cervinae	Cervus	Cervus elephus	red deer
			Cervus canadensis	wapiti, American elk
		Dama	Dama dama	fallow deer
	Odocoileinae	Capreolus	Capreolus capreolus	roe deer
		Odocoileus	Odocoileus hemionus	mule deer, blacktailed deer
			Odocoileus virginianus	whitetailed deer
	Rangiferinae	Rangifer	Rangifer tarandus	reindeer, caribou

Source: *The Whitehead Encyclopedia of Deer*, G. Kenneth Whitehead.

ANTLERS AND HORNS

Antlers must not be confused with horns, although deer antlers are often incorrectly called horns. The horns of bighorn sheep, mountain goats, musk oxen, bison, and antelope, all of which may share deer country in North America, are never shed. Composed of a material called keratin (found in claws, hooves, and fingernails) rather than bone, horns continue to grow as long as the animal lives. American antelope do shed the outer black sheath of the permanent horn every winter. Four months later it is completely replaced.

But what exactly are antlers? The answer is simple: pure bone. It is, in fact, the fastest bone growth known to science. In just three or four summer months, an Alaskan moose can grow a huge rack of antlers equal in weight to the skeleton of a normal adult human.

In most male deer the first antlers appear during the animal's second spring or summer. They are cast from six to nine months later. New antlers grow and are discarded each year as long as the deer lives.

No two sets of antlers are exactly the same in size, weight, or shape. If the deer is healthy and if its nutrition is adequate or better, each succeeding set of antlers will be larger than the previous year's until the deer passes its prime. After that the antlers may gradually become smaller. Depending on its species and range, an animal's "prime" falls sometime between its fourth and tenth years of age. But antler size is never an accurate indicator of a deer's age. Only a careful examination of the deer's teeth can determine how long it has lived.

As a deer's antlers increase in size over the seasons, the general conformation and any individual irregularities will remain somewhat the same. Any distortion resulting from an injury to the antler or antler base (pedicle) will reappear in all subsequent sets of antlers. However, if an aberration is due to an accident occurring early in the antler's yearly growth—if a deer hits its antler tip on a tree limb, for example—that irregularity may not be repeated in later racks. A keen or serious observer in the field can quickly identify many individual males from year to year from just a good look at the antlers.

The conventional wisdom not too long ago was that warm days and the accompanying thawing of the winter landscape triggered the growth of white-tailed deer bucks' antlers in the animals' more northern range. But now we know that no matter how unseasonably warm or cold, the increasing daylight hours of spring alone cause new antlers to emerge from their pedicles and begin to grow. Researchers have learned that antlers do not begin to grow as long as bucks are kept indoors in darkness. Once started, growth stops when the males are confined to unlit quarters. In the tropics, antler growth can begin at any time of year because there are only slight, if any, seasonal changes in the hours of daylight.

GROWTH AND DEVELOPMENT

Antler development in male deer is programmed even before birth. While still in the mother's womb, pedicles atop the tiny skull begin to develop. Later, after birth, these will appear as cowlicks in the forehead hair of male fawns and calves. These pedicles become the connectors between the deer's skull and the antler bone. Researchers have learned that a deer's

This woodland caribou female, nursing a calf, sports small antlers, here in the velvet.

ribs become brittle throughout the antler-growing season, when it borrows calcium and other minerals from its ribs and sternum to supply the growing antlers. Although antlers are "live" as long as they are growing, they "die" and harden when increasing testosterone levels cause the growth to stop.

Most often, the young deer's antlers will begin growing during the first year. Throughout its growth, every antler is covered with a brown skin that looks like staghorn sumac, feels like suede, and is called velvet. This velvet is a modified extension of the skin on the deer's head and is the only regenerating skin known in mammals. The rapidly growing antler bone receives nourishment through tiny blood vessels in that velvet covering and inside the antler itself, which is warm to the touch. The short delicate velvet hairs that cover live antlers as they grow act as feelers (like a cat's whiskers). They are very sensitive to touch and can warn a deer of any obstacles in its path. This prevents collisions and possible injury to the eyes and developing antlers. Male Cervidae seem to have a special ability to judge the size and shape of their own antlers. That means animals with even the largest antlers can travel quickly through heavy cover with

surprisingly little antler damage, or even contact. A fleeing elk, for example, seems able to calculate exactly how much clearance he needs between trees to escape, and whether tilting his head will allow his antlers to pass. He retains this "knowledge" even after the velvet peels away. It is finally shed when the antler bone ceases to grow and hardens, and the velvet is no longer needed. The bare antler, which appears when the velvet is shed, is smooth and tough enough to withstand the powerful impact and stress produced when males use their racks in combat.

Because of their great abundance and economic value worldwide, the Cervidae (especially in North America and Europe) have been the subject of more research than any other wildlife category. Most wildlife biologists now agree that two main factors, nutrition and heredity, determine how fast and how large antlers grow. Biologists in Texas determined that not only is the basic conformation inherited, but so are drop tines, forked brow tines, forked main points, and roughness at the base. Beyond that, there is wide disagreement on which—nutrition or heredity—is more important, and how much more. Recently many have raised questions about the possibly severe

In early autumn a large mule deer buck emerges from dark woods into bright sunlight, revealing that he either has suffered an injury to an antler or has a glandular problem.

effect of air and water pollution—especially that caused by pesticides—on antler development. Antler defects are turning up more frequently in agricultural areas where chemicals are heavily applied. Some researchers believe that hunting pressure, especially prolonged trophy hunting, is a strong consideration in antler development. Removing too many of the largest males year after year is detrimental, they say, to the population as a whole. Others dismiss this theory.

A few facts are not in dispute. Good nutrition early in a male deer's life is essential if that animal is ever to carry a beautiful, impressive rack. Study after study has shown that undernourished fawns develop smaller-than-average pedicles, and this limits eventual antler growth and size. The opposite is also true: Large pedicles permit fast growth of heavy antlers.

The largest antlers of all belonged to *Megaceros giganteus,* the long-extinct Irish or giant elk of the northern European tundra. It carried palmate antlers that measured more than ten feet (3 m) from tip to tip. The largest antlers of any living species belong to the moose of Alaska and the Yukon, with a maximum antler spread of about seven feet (2.1 m). The smallest living deer is the pudu of South America. These bucks stand barely fifteen inches (38 cm) high and grow spike antlers only three or four inches (7.5–10 cm) long.

CONFORMISTS AND NONCONFORMISTS
In what are usually called typical or normal racks, the opposing antlers are symmetrical or very nearly so.

ARCHITECTURE
The architecture or natural conformation of antlers varies greatly from species to species. Some are modest and fairly simple, consisting of the two opposite main beams that originate at the skull pedicle, with only a single tine or fork. Others are elaborate and massive, with very heavy beams, branches, and multiple tines. Moose and fallow deer grow palmate or leaf-shaped antlers. Caribou grow brow tines, which extend forward over the face beyond the nose and may become shovel-shaped.

One side nearly mirrors the other: The main beams and opposite tines are approximately the same thickness, length, and curvature and carry an equal number of points. The bulls and bucks of different races and localities often tend to have a conformation unique to their area. No doubt it is a matter of heredity and semi-isolation. Mule deer in one area, for instance, may have antlers that grow high above the skull, while mule deer in another region have antlers whose growth tends instead to be more lateral.

Then there are the nontypicals, or malformed antlers, which often as not are more massive than typicals of any given species. These are asymmetrical, with unequal numbers of points per side or strange, twisted conformations. There is no way to describe some nontypicals except as heavy masses of bone. Some of these are huge and extremely impressive. The antlers seem to have exploded from the skull, often exhibiting two to three times the bone mass of a deer of similar age and size living in the same environment.

Nontypical antlers may result from injury to the antler or pedicle early in development, screw worm infestations, or other causes biologists have not yet identified. Injuries to the animal elsewhere in the body may also affect antler shape and growth. A moose that suffered a broken leg in a collision with a car thereafter grew only a stunted antler on the injured side even though the leg healed completely.

While whitetail deer antlers are classified as typical or nontypical, often whitetail racks are further separated into three categories of conformation types, all very descriptive: "wide horn," "high horn," and "basket horn."

THE WHY OF ANTLERS
But why do deer grow—or need—antlers in the first place? The most obvious answer might be for offense and defense: to confront and defeat rivals during the breeding season and as protection against predators. It is true that Cervidae males do fight, occasionally savagely, as some of the photos in this book show, but their antlers' most vital use may not be as weapons.

Consider, for example, the fact that most deer do not carry their hardened antlers when, if their major purpose is protection, they need them most—when predators are most likely to be a serious threat.

KEEPING SCORE

Humans' natural competitiveness have led us to devise systems to accurately measure, score, and compare the largest trophy heads.

The first scoring system originated with Rowland Ward, an old prestigious firm of taxidermists in London. Beginning early in the 1900s, the company published record books listing the world's largest horns and antlers. North American species were included through the 1928 edition, but were unaccountably omitted after that. Some other ranking systems were devised, but all fell short. They considered only the length and/or spread of antler beams and did not really evaluate the overall excellence—the mass and attractiveness—of a set of antlers. In 1930 the Conseil International de la Chasse was formed in Paris, first as a big game conservation organization and later to record outstanding trophies taken worldwide. The C.I.C. published the book Game Trophies of the World in 1981, listing top trophies mostly by the length of the main antler beams or horns.

Almost a century earlier, in 1887, conservationist and U.S. president Theodore Roosevelt invited a group of American outdoorsmen to his home, Sagamore Hill, New York, to discuss forming a society dedicated to the highest standards of sportsmanship and to the preservation of large game in the United States. This meeting led to the formation of the Boone and Crockett Club (see address in "Organizations"). Since then the club has sponsored numerous conservation projects and has been a strong factor in passing sound environmental legislation. Membership rolls have included such respected names as Aldo Leopold, George Bird Grinnell, Ding Darling, Gifford Pinchot, William Hornaday, and William Sheldon. But the club is best known as the inventor of a trophy scoring system for big game animals and as a repository for big game records. Almost all of the largest antlers taken or found in North America during the past one hundred years or so have been measured and duly recorded by Boone and Crockett official scorers. In 1932, Boone and Crockett published its first Records of North American Big Game. The tenth edition was printed in 1993. It lists the dimensions, location, and date of capture of about eight thousand of the largest Cervidae antlers in any public or private collection.

Under the Boone and Crockett method, a male deer's antlers are scored as the sum of the following dimensions

(measured down to 1/16 inch [0.16 cm]): the length of the two main beams, length of all normal tines or branches, the greatest inside distance between the right and left main antler beams, and the largest circumference of the main beams. The total of these in inches is called the preliminary score.

If it is a typical head, deductions are then made for any difference in length between the two main antler beams. Deductions are also made for any abnormal points. If there are four points on one side and five on the other, the length of that extra point is subtracted from the preliminary score to determine the final score. Malformed or nontypical racks are scored the same way, except that all points (tines) no matter how many or where located, are measured and counted in the final score. Although this Boone and Crockett measuring system was invented to score North American species (horned as well as antlered game), it can be applied to (and is arguably the best scoring system yet devised for) any and all of the world's other deer.

A somewhat similar scoring system has been devised by the Safari Club International (see address in "Organizations"), which publishes an International Record Book of Trophy Animals.

The Pope and Young Club (see address in "Organizations"), which maintains records of trophies taken with bow

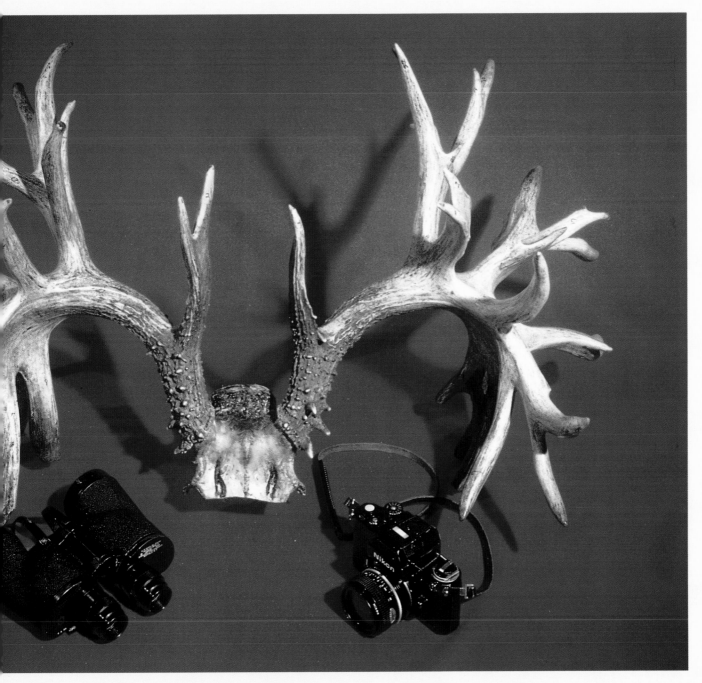

These antlers, found in 1981 in St. Louis County, Missouri, property of the Missouri Department of Conservation, are recognized in Boone and Crockett's 1993 record book as the largest of all known whitetail antlers.

and arrow, uses the Boone and Crockett system. So does the Longhunter Society (see address in "Organizations"), which keeps records for antique firearms trophies. It is generally agreed that the Boone and Crockett scoring system is the best and fairest for measuring and rating antlers.

There is even a mushrooming interest in searching for and collecting cast or shed antlers. Some of the largest deer antlers known are such "pickups." The North American

Shed Hunters Club (see address in "Organizations") holds an annual show and competition for antlers picked up during invigorating winter expeditions. Replicating trophy antlers in plastic has also become an important hobby and business. The best-known replicator is Klaus Lebrecht of Ellsworth, Wisconsin, who has produced limited editions of some of the most famous deer heads, often from sheds.

Pages 22–25: *Antlers should never be confused with horns. Antlers are shed and replaced every year; horns continue to grow as long as the animal lives. But a number of horned mammals share the range of antlered animals, have evolved with them, and often compete with them. The Arctic range of the muskox* **(facing page)** *overlaps with that of Barren Ground caribou. In many mountainous areas bighorn sheep* **(right)** *live with elk, mule deer, and occasionally with moose. It is not unusual to find mountain goats* **(above)** *living in the same lofty areas as mule deer, especially bachelor muley bucks in summertime.*

Bison **(page 24)** *share Yellowstone and Theodore Roosevelt national parks and other sanctuaries of the West with elk, mule deer, and whitetailed deer. The Dall or white sheep* **(page 25 top)** *of Alaska and the Yukon share areas with Barren Ground caribou. Both muleys and whitetails can be seen in the same pastures with pronghorn antelope* **(page 25 bottom)**, *at times very close together.*

That critical time is when the deer are still very young and again each winter after the antlers are shed. Also, if antlers are for defense, why don't females have them? I once saw a whitetail buck with good antlers beset by a pack of feral dogs. In defense, the deer slashed at its attackers with its front hooves and not its antlers as one might have expected.

Bucks and bulls seem to depend mostly on their antlers to determine ranking or dominance in a herd or a territory simply by displaying them well. The largest, healthiest males with the most impressive racks usually do most of the breeding, but they are rarely forced to engage in any serious combat to do so. Just displaying their antlers, while making proper body and head movements, is enough to intimidate potential rivals.

Antlers probably also serve as attractors or advertisement to females. Keen observers have often noted that females in heat or estrus tend to prefer mates with heavier racks.

Some other observations should be made. Males may recognize one another more readily by their antlers than by scent. When familiar males meet, they often have already established who is dominant and have no need for a contest. Unfamiliar males may posture or spar to settle the open question of rank. Numerous experiments with captive herds of different species have shown that when the antlers of an established dominant herd male have been removed, the de-antlered males were soon challenged by other males who no longer recognized or feared them.

THE EVOLUTION OF STYLE

Whatever their uses, the antler designs of different species have evolved over the millennia in adaptation to environment. There is a definite relationship between structure or shape of the antlers and habitat. A whitetail buck's antlers curve forward and slightly inward to protect its eyes as the animal bounds through dense brush. The antlers of elk and their close Eurasian relatives seem perfectly designed to facilitate their movements through mountain forest foliage. One of the best examples of antler adaptation to environment occurs in moose. The woodland subspecies have generally parallel and more upright antler palms, while those of tundra or Alaskan moose are more widespread and flattened. The latter are less resistant to the

constant winds of more open spaces.

Every male deer follows its own annual cycle, dropping its antlers at about the same time each year. New growth begins surprisingly soon, usually within a week or two. When antlers are shed, they do not survive long in the wild. The bone is full of calcium, phosphorus, and other mineral salts that a great variety of rodents, from mice and voles to squirrels and

porcupines, need for nutrition. Once on the ground, the sheds are gnawed by these creatures. Several species of deer have also been observed eating cast antlers. Sun and rain soon bleach, soften, and erode away any uneaten portions, and thus antlers eventually return to the soil. Their minerals will supply nourishment to plants eaten by another generation of deer to grow antlers. That is the cycle of nature.

Grand Teton National Park, Wyoming. Antelope often graze across Antelope Flats in the foreground, occasionally with moose, while elk and mule deer inhabit the foothills in the background.

LIVING IN A NATURAL BALANCE

All of the antlered species in this book are important members, and often the largest members, of their natural ecosystems—of wild communities of plants and animals that form a network of interdependence. Originally these ecosystems included predators. Although the meat-eaters lived by killing and eating other species within the ecosystem, including the antlered ones, the two groups were entirely compatible.

Wolves and caribou, for example, evolved together over many thousands of years. Deer and mountain lions developed parallel lives. These two still share wilderness areas across North America and to varying degrees actually depend on one another.

I cannot emphasize that relationship enough. The predators require the wild deer and other creatures for the calories they need to survive. And perhaps surprisingly, the reverse is also true. If their numbers are not controlled, deer and elk herds soon expand beyond the ability of the land to support them. In time this leads to complete ruin of the ecosystem. Wherever predators have been eliminated—as they too often have been, especially in Europe—it has been necessary to "manage" (harvest) the deer either by

sport or commercial hunting, or by some less attractive means.

The ideal situation is to maintain a healthy population of both antlered animals and predators that is large enough to allow some regulated hunting of each. That is perfectly possible today through modern, scientific game management. Sound management also makes possible the raising and taking of bigger and better antlered trophies.

The bottom line is that the meat-eaters are extremely important, and not only in wildlife conservation. No photography, hunting, backpacking, or hiking trip in wilderness is ever exactly the same where no predators lurk.

Many different predators, from red foxes to Alaskan brown bears, have some impact at some time on the Cervidae. The senses of sight, smell, and sound are at least as keen in predators as in prey. Most are also agile, stealthy, swift footed, and good swimmers. Still, some predators such as foxes, fishers, wolverines, or lynx are either so small or so slow that they can capture only the youngest, smallest deer. Others are important only as recyclers of carcasses left by other predators. All must be considered among the most interesting and vital animals living on earth.

Facing page: A stunning view of the Absaroka-Beartooth Wilderness, overlooking the Yellowstone River valley, Montana. The authors have seen or photographed all of the North American deer species except caribou in this scene at one time or another. *Above:* Elk share the range of the National Bison Range, Montana, with bison and other ungulates. *Right:* Wolves are persistent hunters that can run long distances, covering vast territories in search of prey. Wolves traditionally preyed on all of the Cervidae — and still do so wherever the wolves still survive. Here, wolves feed on a bull elk carcass. Bulls, weakened by the rut (during which they do not feed), are most susceptible to predators in winter.

Above: *Antlers are subject to injuries of many kinds. This Alberta bull elk may have been struck by a car. Other than the deformed antler, it appeared to be healthy.* **Left:** *Pedicles, shown here on this caribou calf, become the connectors between the deer's skull and the antler bone.* **Facing page:** *Huge as they already are (here photographed in mid-August), the antlers of this splendid Columbian whitetail buck, a subspecies named for its range in Washington state, may still grow a little larger.*

All photos: *These photos show various stages of elk antler growth—from the nubbins that usually appear in April after the old antlers are cast, to the super trophy antlers. A twelve-point (six per side) bull is considered "normal."*

Facing page top: *A mule deer buck in its prime with an excellent, typical rack of antlers.* Facing page bottom: *Antler bone receives nourishment through blood vessels in the velvet and inside the antler itself.* Above: *I'm sure this is one of the largest typical racks on a live, free-roaming whitetailed deer ever photographed. It would score about 190 points by the Boone and Crockett system. This buck was photographed in November 1993 on a ranch in north-central Texas where limited trophy hunting is permitted.* Above right: *This mule deer buck has almost perfectly symmetrical antlers—a typical specimen. Its neck is swollen for the rut.* Right: *A very good example of nontypical antlers in a mule deer buck.*

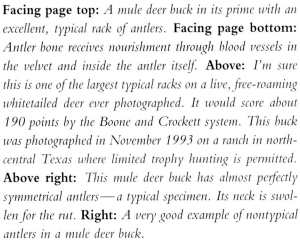

Above left: *Closeups of the strange antler growth of a Missouri whitetail buck. It's impossible to say, for certain, exactly what caused this unique formation.* **Above:** *A mule buck uses antlers to try to dislodge a tick from its rump.* **Left:** *The blood-colored antlers of this Barren Ground caribou bull in Alaska match the scarlet vegetation of autumn in the Alaska Range.*

Top: *An Alberta mule deer buck, with antlers half-grown and in the velvet, loses the velvet early in September.* **Center:** *This arctic ground squirrel has been gnawing on the antlers of a winter- or wolf-killed bull moose.* **Bottom:** *This antler was shed in early April by a small bull elk. There is still blood where the antler separated from the pedicle.*

These photos contrast the conformation of antlers of Wyoming or Shiras moose to those of Alaskan moose. The Shiras bull **(left)** *is more a forest mammal and its antlers tend to grow upward. The Alaskan bull* **(above)** *lives in more open landscapes and its antlers have evolved into a more flattened shape to better cope with the steady winds.*

Two absolutely outstanding woodland caribou bulls, one wearing the velvet antlers of summer **(above)**, *the other with antlers polished and ready for the breeding season* **(right)**.

MOOSE

Compared to other large creatures of the earth, and even to some other species of deer, moose, *Alces alces*, are doing fairly well despite the death of long-distance travelers, such as the "vagabond Minnesota moose" and the evening news star from Massachusetts, and of those that wander every winter from evergreen forests into towns. Their range may not be as extensive now as it was a century and more ago, but with minor fluctuations, their populations are fairly stable. During the late 1980s and early 1990s, they became numerous enough in New England to justify an open hunting season in Maine. An estimated one hundred live in Michigan's Upper Peninsula and northern Minnesota. Significant numbers of moose occupy about two-thirds of Canada and almost all of Alaska, as well as the Rocky Mountain region from Alberta southward to northern Utah and Colorado. The Alaskan population is somewhere between 100,000 and 200,000.

A very large bull moose, photographed in Alaska as the velvet is shedding. These antlers are the heaviest, bulkiest headgear carried by any animal.

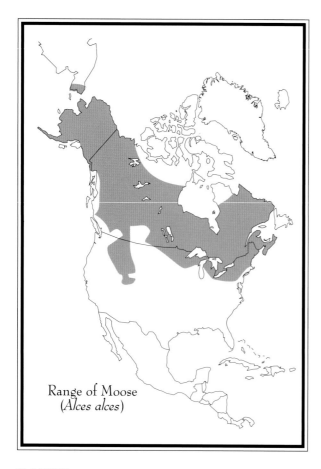

Range of Moose
(*Alces alces*)

RANGE

When we speak of North American moose, we are really speaking of four subspecies that are not greatly different in appearance. Bulls of *Alces alces gigas* of Alaska and the Yukon stand an average two feet (61 cm) higher at the shoulder than the smallest, *A.a. americana* of the eastern third of Canada and New England. In between are *A.a. andersoni* of central and western Canada, the most widespread race, and *A.a. shirasi* of the northern Rocky Mountains, which has the smallest range. The last was named for George Shiras, a pioneering wildlife photographer who probably was the first to take pictures of several species (including the moose) at night with a flash. Most of our own personal experiences have been with this last subspecies, which frequently wandered over our property and shared our view of the Tetons when we lived in Jackson Hole, Wyoming.

No other living animals carry as much "baggage"—horns or antlers—on their heads as male moose. A number of bulls have been taken in Alaska with racks exceeding six feet (1.8 m) in total spread. One of these, taken near Redoubt Bay in 1958, was

only inches short of seven feet (2.1 m) wide. The Boone and Crockett record antlers, taken near McGrath, Alaska, measured seventy-seven inches (195.6 cm) tip to tip and had thirty-four points.

Two other species of moose, called elk or elch, inhabit the Old World. *A.a. alces* ranges across Scandinavia and northern Russia. *A.a. cameloides* lives or once lived in Siberia, Manchuria, and Mongolia. In the field they very much resemble North American moose, and it would be difficult to distinguish between the two.

BEAUTY IN MOTION

Too often moose are described as ungainly or ugly or both. But anyone familiar with them knows better. The moose I see occasionally on Suce Creek near our home, like all others, are handsome and perfectly adapted survivors. It isn't ungainly to be able to plod through deeper snow or to wade more easily through muck-bottomed marshes than any of the other Cervidae we will meet in this book. Those long, powerful legs are a definite asset.

Despite its size and the great antlers of some males, a moose depends on its legs and long strides to quickly escape trouble—usually predators, but at times rivals. The individual that stomps away through a dry forest, snapping off tree limbs and crushing brush underfoot, can also sneak away silently, almost ghostlike through the same timber, without ever scraping an antler tip.

The long face and overhanging muzzle of a moose is perfectly suited to the species's needs. That large muzzle allows a moose to neatly, even delicately, strip tender green leaves from branches and willow shoots. Consider also how a moose can feed selectively on submerged aquatic vegetation, wading belly deep in a marsh or beaver pond, while keeping its eyes well above the water line. That way a cow can watch out for her calf and any potential predators as well.

Next to its long legs and drooping visage, a moose's hide may be the most noticeable feature. The deep, heavy body is covered with long outer hair that is dark brown or black. The legs tend to be lighter, usually gray, especially on the insides. During the most terrible winters, while the dark outer hair absorbs heat from even meager sunlight, an undercoat of finer body hair insulates and helps ensure survival. Time

Above: *A Shiras bull in Wyoming browses on lush green vegetation of summer. It is the least stressful time of year for moose.* **Right:** *The typical environment, flooded by beavers, of moose in Grand Teton National Park, Wyoming.*

and again during Montana and Wyoming winters we have seen moose, even calves, bedded for days in snow that almost covered them until the blizzard passed. Except possibly for caribou, moose are better equipped to withstand long periods of bitter cold than any other Cervidae.

SOCIAL BEHAVIOR

A common misconception about moose is that they are solitary mammals. Compared to elk or caribou (both herd species), probably they are. But we have found two or more moose together far more often than we have encountered single animals. Cow moose, for example, are almost always accompanied by calves. During the rut, a cow is likely to be followed not only by her calf or calves, but by a number of suitors. One autumn afternoon in Grand Teton National Park, we found one popular female in estrus surrounded by eight bulls and her twin calves. We estimated that altogether the newly polished antlers worn by these males would have weighed almost three hundred pounds (135 kg).

Bachelor groups, especially of *shiras* males, are common in winter. One late November day in 1975, we counted thirty-three moose, mostly bulls, herded together in one area of about fifty acres (20 hectares) near Moran, Wyoming. However, such large herds are uncommon anywhere, anytime.

MATING

The rut is the most exciting time in the annual cycle of the moose, or probably of any deer. When summer ends, tolerance among the bulls also ends. Just as the last bloodied velvet is being rubbed from antlers, they begin posturing, jousting, and testing one another. They also begin the single-minded search for females, grunting all the way.

Courtship can occasionally be a sedate affair with one bull standing near to guard a cow, following her almost in lockstep, until mating finally takes place. But more often there is competition and that results in two or more bulls in attendance, with the matter of dominance still to be settled. It may come down to a noisy, head-to-head clash between the two top contenders. These are almost always the two with the heaviest antlers. I once saw a pair of battlers lock antlers during such a contest, but they somehow sepa-

rated in a few minutes. Only very rarely are they permanently locked, though with fatal results.

Estrus lasts about twenty-four hours in September or October. Both sexes are capable of breeding when one and one-half years old, and most cows have calves when two and one-half years old. When males breed, if at all, depends on circumstance, on being

---

MOOSE ENCOUNTERS

It is an understatement to say that mother moose are protective of their calves. Plenty of hikers, backpackers, and anglers traveling moose country have been threatened or even treed by angry mamas. Floating a wilderness river in Ontario, fortyish Al Forsky and his teenage son were dunked in icy water by an enraged cow when they accidentally drifted too near her small calf standing on the bank. The female jumped into their inflatable raft and punctured it.

Some moose especially seem to dislike small dogs yapping at them. Not far from Anchorage, Alaska, sixty-six-year-old Anisha McCormick was trampled to death when she apparently tried to rescue her dogs from a bull moose in the rutting season.

Louise Lecoeuvre was snowshoeing near her Alpine, Wyoming, home when a moose suddenly appeared from nowhere and ran over the top of her. It happened so suddenly that she still does not know if it was a bull or a cow. The animal punched one hoof through her snowshoe webbing and dragged the unfortunate woman about thirty feet (9.1 m) before it extricated itself, leaving her in a snowdrift with cracked bones and ribs. Lecoeuvre's husband later found her hypothermic and helpless. He got her to the hospital in Jackson Hole where she eventually recovered. A year later she was snowshoeing again and bears no grudges whatever against the moose.

Facing page: *An Alaskan bull moose in its velvet browses on tender green willow under a low summer sun.*

dominant, and on appearing at the right place at the right time. After eight months' gestation, cows give birth to single calves, occasionally to twins. In Denali National Park, Alaska, we saw a cow with triplets, two of which were subsequently caught by grizzly bears. The next year she again had triplets, but this second time around, all were eaten by the bears, despite the mother's charges to protect them.

Moose are not only the biggest members of the deer family—they are also the ones that most deserve our watchfulness.

The Hayden Valley of the Yellowstone River is a good place to find moose browsing on vegetation on any summer evening.

VAGABOND MOOSE TAILS

One October morning in 1985 Jack Whitman, a biologist in Glenallen, Alaska, received a telephone call from conservation officer Joe D'Amico. Two bull moose that had been fighting were found with their antlers locked. Since both animals would die unless soon separated, Whitman collected his immobilizing equipment and a saw. Then he and D'Amico prepared to fly in a light plane over the wilderness area to locate the moose. After a careful search they were unable to spot the animals and figured they had somehow separated.

The foul weather that is endemic to the fall season in that part of Alaska kept the men grounded for two days, and they more or less forgot about the moose mission. Six days later they received another report that the bulls were still in the area and still with antlers locked. This time the men got a more detailed description of the site and they soon found the combatants.

The weak and bedraggled animals were still standing, joined together, although they had no water, food, or rest for over a week. Whitman wondered whether a normal full dose of his immobilizing drug would be too much for the weakened animals. He decided to try a half dose, and while the two continued to struggle, Whitman shot a drug-filled dart into the larger bull's rump. In a few minutes it was down, pulling the other bull's head down, too. Next he shot the other moose, but this dart seemed to have no effect.

Whitman and D'Amico decided to saw anyway and after a few tense minutes had severed one of the antlers near its base (the loss of an antler posed no threat to the moose's future). For the first time since they had become entangled, the animals were able to raise their heads. And within five minutes, according to the biologist, both animals were walking, browsing on willows and eyeing one another with hostility. This is an excellent example of the tenacity and endurance of the world's largest deer.

At about the same time, completely across the continent, a young bull moose was spotted in a marsh near Salisbury Beach, Massachusetts, where moose normally are as rare as honest politicians. Later it was seen lumbering through Salisbury across an interstate highway, through a used car lot, and down a railroad track along the Merrimack River. No matter where it was aimed in this densely popu-

lated region, it was headed for trouble. But it wound up in possibly the worst place that a quarter-ton (225-kg) wild animal could: Lowell, Massachusetts. There it immediately attracted the attention of police and firefighters, kids, housewives, and hordes of assorted other curious citizens, plus television crews. What followed — trying to escape in terror from the fire hoses, blinking lights, sirens, and guns — was described on the evening news as "an antlered monster running amok."

Somehow the animal blundered into a canal where a team of "rescuers" hog-tied and blindfolded it. They then loaded the moose into a pickup trailer and drove off toward open country in New Hampshire. Not yet to its destination, the young bull crashed out of the trailer and made a spectacular getaway.

The sad tale continued when the moose was next seen attempting to cross a foggy interstate highway in Vermont and was killed by a car. This incident well illustrates the unpredictability and wanderlust of some male moose. But this Massachusetts bull, believed to have come from Maine, does not hold any mileage records. Far from it.

Autumn seems to be the travel time for bull moose. Sometime in fall of 1976, another bull began legging it from Lake Superior southward through Minnesota, carrying a new rack of antlers. By December it had reached the Des Moines River in northern Iowa where it remained until the velvet was rubbed from his second set of antlers. Unlike the moose in Massachusetts, this one made quite a few human friends while in Iowa. Some were genuinely sorry when he vanished in the fall of 1977. Most figured he left to search for female companionship. Before Christmas the bull was seen crossing into northern Missouri. During 1978, the moose was sighted in scattered areas and appeared on television news a time or two. It was last seen alive in February 1979 near the Mississippi River at Louisiana, Missouri.

A month or so later Marion Trayner was scouting a southern Missouri woods for a place to hunt wild turkeys. But what he found was a pair of shed moose antlers that would (with the skull) have measured forty-one inches (104 cm) wide. Almost certainly these belonged to the Minnesota vagabond, three years and about fifteen hundred miles (2,400 km) from home.

Above: *An excellent specimen of a Shiras bull, its antlers free of velvet, in Grand Teton National Park, Wyoming.*
Right: *A Shiras cow and her nearly full-grown calf winter together in Jackson Hole, Wyoming. The habitat here can support a good population of wintering moose.*

An Alaskan moose cow and a calf cross an inlet of Wonder Lake in Denali National Park and Preserve in late summer. Caribou also pass this point during migrations.

Left: *An Alaskan bull moose, its velvet shedding.* **Facing page:** *A critical time for moose survival anywhere is winter, when food is scarce. Animals must conserve energy and strength, but also must travel to find browse.*

Facing page: *Soon after the bulls shed their velvet, the question of dominance will be settled by noisy, head-to-head clashes between the two top contenders. The winners usually have the larger antlers.* **Right:** *Fireweed brightens meadows of Kaflia Bay, Katmai National Park, Alaska, where moose graze in midsummer along with brown bears.*

Right: *In summer, moose frequent the areas around beaver ponds such as this in Elk Island National Park, Alberta.* **Overleaf:** *Young Alaskan bull moose spar just prior to the rut on Igloo Flat in Denali National Park, Alaska.*

ELK

No matter what the size of the antlers, nor whether it is male or female, the American elk, *Cervus canadensis,* also called wapiti, is a splendid, resilient animal and a living symbol of our wilderness.

Five very similar subspecies are recognized: *C.c. nelsoni* from the New Mexico Rockies northward to Alberta; *C.c. manitobensis* of the Duck Hills in Saskatchewan and Manitoba; and *C.c. roosevelti* of the coastal ranges in Oregon, Washington, and British Columbia. Two others, *C.c. canadensis* and *C.c. merriami,* are extinct. It is believed that one race or another once inhabited almost all of the United States (except the deep South) and southern Canada. Many other species and subspecies of the genus *Cervus* live elsewhere in Europe and Asia, and a few have been introduced elsewhere. All wapiti (this name originating from a Native American word) inhabit some of the most beautiful mountain land left in the world.

The American elk, also called wapiti, inhabits ranges scattered across the northwestern United States and in Canada.

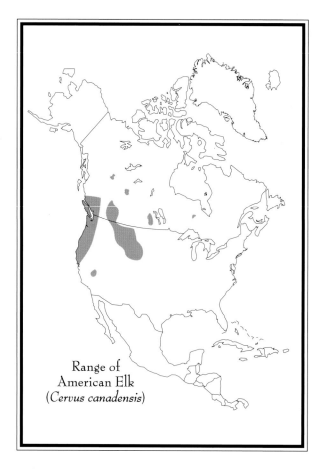

Range of
American Elk
(*Cervus canadensis*)

COLORS OF SPRING

Every May there is a renewal of life in these mountains of western North America. Wildflowers bloom and blow in the first warm winds of the year. The first leaves appear on willows at lower elevations. Soon the cottonwoods and quaking aspens also are a bright, new green. Mornings are still cold and sometimes frosty, but the bite of winter is gone. Cow elk that were bred in September and October, eight and one-half months earlier, drift away from their herds and in seclusion give birth to single calves. On two or three occasions we have seen twins.

The spotted, reddish brown youngsters weigh about thirty-five pounds (15.75 kg) at birth, and for a while their coats offer fairly good camouflage in high country forest glades. Still they are vulnerable and spend much of their first weeks bedded down. The mothers feed some distance away and return every few hours to nurse them. Eventually the restive calves follow their mothers and rejoin loose herds in their summer, high-altitude ranges.

One morning during a trout-fishing pack trip into the Yellowstone backcountry, outfitter Gene

Wade and I sat on a hillside soaking up the delicious early summer sunshine. On a slope just opposite us, seven cow elk grazed on the nutritious new vegetation. Their calves ran, played, and butted one another. Suddenly one cow barked and instantly all the gamboling stopped. The calves, now motionless, blended into the earth.

A moment later we saw the reason for the alarm: A grizzly bear with a cub made her way between us and the elk, following a game trail. The bruins appeared to see neither the elk nor us, but were probably acutely aware of both.

The next day, riding about two miles (3.2 km) from that area, Gene dismounted and focused his binoculars on a dark blotch several hundred yards away. Seen through the field glasses, that smudge proved to be two grizzlies, probably that same mother and cub, eating an elk calf. An elk cow stood watching them from atop a ridge nearby.

Bears, mountain lions, coyotes, and wolves today prey on calves as they have for thousands of years. But scientific investigations have proved that all this predation combined is not a serious factor in overall elk numbers. Rather it is the quality of the environment that is the determining or limiting factor.

DIET

Elk are both grazers (grass-eaters) and browsers (shrub-eaters). And they eat a great variety of plants. Like all the other Cervidae, they are also ruminants. The plant material they consume is digested in a four-chambered stomach. The unchewed vegetation goes into a first stomach, or rumen, where it is stored. After feeding, when they rest in a standing position or (more often) bedded down, the food is regurgitated from the rumen as cud, which the animal chews and then swallows again. Digestion is completed in the other stomachs.

Elk must eat great amounts of food to extract the energy and strength they need. Cows require plenty to produce milk for the growing calves as well as for nourishing themselves. Bulls require an abundance of green matter to grow antlers. Ruminating allows all to do this more safely: to spend less time feeding out in the open. Later, in winter, they can save energy by feeding in cold wind for a shorter time, then ruminating while bedded down in shelter.

This newly born elk calf, less than an hour old, is still wet and unsteady on its feet. The cow is tired from the ordeal. Mothers and calves remain close together during the calves' first summer, and the young continue to nurse for three to four months.

The chewing is done efficiently by rows of molars on both top and bottom jaws, plus incisors on the front of the lower jaw. All elk also have canine teeth on either side of the upper jaw. Whereas the canines of meat-eaters are pointed, those of elk are rounded, very hard, and known as "elk ivory." In fact the demand for this ivory for watch fobs and other jewelry was so great fifty years ago that thousands of animals were slaughtered just to retrieve their canine teeth. Native Americans of the area also considered the ivory to have great value. At the fine Whitney Museum in Cody, Wyoming, a buckskin dress completely covered with elk ivories is on display.

SOCIAL BEHAVIOR

Bulls spend western summers alone or compatibly in small bachelor "clubs." If rainfall has been adequate and the summer range has not been overgrazed by domestic livestock, a healthy Rocky Mountain bull can reach from five hundred pounds (225 kg) to nearly a half-ton (450 kg) and stand four to five feet (1.2–1.5 m) high at the shoulder. Adult cows are somewhat smaller, weighing from four hundred to a little over six hundred pounds (180–270 kg).

Herding is common among Cervidae, and elk certainly are herd animals. The "safety in numbers" concept is the reason most often cited for herding, as more eyes and ears are on the alert for predators. But in the case of elk, some biologists are not sold on that theory. No matter though, because when summer begins to blend into autumn, all begin the annual group trek out of the high country toward winter range.

Again there is debate over whether tradition, weather (especially snowfall), availability of food, or some combination of these factors triggers the migration. Particularly in regions where there is little or no hunting pressure, as in national parks, by early to mid-September the herds of cows with calves and the summer-fattened bulls come together in the same

This elk calf is less than two weeks old, but already is steady afoot and fairly agile. But it is still vulnerable to wolves, bears, and cougars if not protected by its mother.

places—the same rutting areas, as one biologist calls them—at virtually the same time each fall. What follows is the most exciting period in the elk's life cycle, both for the animals and for the humans who watch, photograph, and study the fascinating spectacle.

MATING

We always set aside September to visit Yellowstone in Wyoming or Jasper National Park in Alberta, or both. Photographing the rut year after year does not become, as one would suppose, tedious or repetitious. I remember especially one year when the rut seemed to be especially intense. On September 10 in 1975, Peggy and I had pitched our tent in the Norris Campground in Yellowstone National Park. From our site on a low bluff we overlooked the Gibbon River and a vast, grassy meadow where about thirty elk had already congregated. One not especially large bull with antlers of average size seemed to have taken command of the herd. He had rounded up about twenty females into a harem.

The last sound we heard that evening, after crawling into heavy sleeping bags and before finally falling asleep, was the bugling of this harem bull. Occasionally it was quiet long enough that I heard him slashing at saplings all around us with his antlers.

Very early in the morning, just before day broke on a landscape silver with frost, the bugling continued. But now the sound was much different. When it was light enough, I unzipped the tent flaps part way to look outside and saw the reason. During the night a changing of the guard had occurred. Not far distant, its body steaming and its breath white, a much larger bull stood urinating on itself. As I watched, still in my sleeping bag, it bugled and then plunged into and across the Gibbon River as if to check out its female inventory. The original harem bull was missing.

While we brewed coffee on a light backpacking stove and wolfed down a cold cereal breakfast, Peggy made another interesting observation. The first bull had not entirely given up. Instead it stood watching the show from the cover of lodgepole pines that bordered the meadow.

By sunrise a contingent of other wildlife photographers had joined us along the Gibbon River. Before mid-morning, all had a chance to shoot a confrontation that may have been a classic. The smaller bull decided to make one last challenge and came charging back. The other met it head on. What followed lasted less than a minute, but plenty of turf was overturned as the two lunged at one another. Mostly I remember the crash and rattle of antlers. Then all at once the smaller bull was running away; the larger followed close behind for a short distance, until it was certain there would be no second attempt. Maybe the most interesting thing is this: Few if any of the cows, grazing all around, even bothered to look up at the violent combat.

As is almost always the case among the herd species, the harem bulls do almost all of the breeding, after fighting for the privilege. Often there are casualties. Antlers sometimes snap, and I have seen some injuries from goring. Rarely (more rarely it seems than in smaller deer) antlers become locked, resulting in two losers rather than one. By the end of the rut, all of the healthy cows have come into estrus and have been bred. By mid-October courtship in the meadows dwindles, ending at about the same time the first heavy snows fall.

A word of caution should be noted. During the rutting seasons in late 1993, a few bulls were acting aggressively toward people in Yellowstone and Jasper parks. A few passing vehicles were punctured by thrust antlers. These may be isolated or aberrant incidents caused when eager wildlife watchers press too close to aroused males. However, the wisest course is always to maintain plenty of distance from any bulls of any species, especially during the rut.

A lone bull patrols a high meadow in fall near Maligne Lake, Jasper National Park, Alberta.

63

Of all native meat-eaters, coyotes have been among the most persecuted by humans. Still, today they prosper almost everywhere in North America. Pictured is a coyote with an elk carcass.

COYOTES: OCCASIONAL PREDATORS

If any predator has been more persecuted in North America than the wolf, and with even less reason, it is the coyote. We have used firearms, aircraft, the deadliest poisons, sophisticated electronics, and even synthetic birth control chemicals to kill coyotes for the past fifty years, and the toll should sicken us. But even though the body count has been high, we have lost the battle. This is one predator more numerous today and with a much greater range across the continent than ever before. Once a western United States resident, the coyote now lives in every state and Canadian province.

Superficially Canis latrans *could be described as a miniature or brush wolf. Adults weigh from twenty-five to forty pounds (11.3–18 kg) and stand approximately two feet (0.6 m) high at the shoulder. Their color varies from light cream in northern specimens to reddish brown along the Texas Gulf Coast.*

Coyotes really are hunters of small game and will catch a deer or antelope fawn at any opportunity. Because almost all fawns are born within one brief period each spring, the numbers overwhelm even the most determined coyote. Very soon the fawns, difficult to find in the first place, are able to outrun the hunters. In addition coyotes must, on occasion, deal with defensive mothers. I have watched the mothers of both mule deer and antelope successfully drive coyotes away from their young.

Certainly studies from southern Texas and the Southwest are worth noting here. Coyote predation on whitetail fawns was much greater on ranches where domestic livestock grazed than where the brush country was managed for and restricted to deer only. Another study revealed that predation by feral hogs was greater than predation by coyotes. In fact coyotes are often blamed when hogs are the true culprits.

WINTER

After the rut the elk herds begin to move toward natural winter ranges or to elk feeding grounds where humans supply hay or pellets. The struggle to survive another winter begins. Some will not make it.

Not all the elk migrate long distances and some do not travel at all. The Roosevelt or Olympic elk of the Pacific Coast shift ranges only slightly as compared to most Rocky Mountain elk. The Tule elk of more temperate California travel even less. Even some Rocky Mountain animals live year-round near the same thermal areas of Yellowstone National Park.

In the main though, winter is an ordeal. Forage intake declines and elk move about only as much as is necessary. Energy and fat reserves accumulated in summer and fall are used up, with some elk losing as much as 15 percent of their body weight by springtime. A heavy snowpack and subzero temperatures take a toll. Predators and parasites (and the resulting loss of hair) contribute to the casualties.

Unlike many of their Cervidae relatives around the world, American elk bulls do not cast their antlers soon after the rut. Nearly all retain them until March, even beyond the vernal equinox when the

Black bears share antler country almost everywhere and have a minor predatory role. This bear is trying to glean nourishment from a desiccated elk skull.

and Europe have always captured deer fawns when they found them. For a short time during the calving season in Yellowstone Park, some grizzlies will actively and deliberately hunt for newly dropped elk calves. But the fact that the Yellowstone elk herd is over-populating park land and devastating some parts of it (thanks in part to the absence of wolves that once roamed there) is evidence that the bears do not catch nearly enough calves.

Most of the predators described here have another, very important role in antler country and that is as recyclers. Whenever a deer dies, no matter what the cause, a bear, coyote, or wolverine will soon locate the carcass. It may find the animal by scent or it may follow the flight of ravens, eagles, and magpies to the spot. When a bear comes upon a dead elk or deer, it will remain with and guard its prize until only the skeleton and antlers are left for other, smaller predators to finish.

For me antler country couldn't possibly be the same without the predators that share it.

BEARS AND ELK

Many of our most memorable days in the field, shooting the antler photos for this book, were those when we also heard the howling of wolves or the haunting song of the coyote family. So also were the exhilarating times when we sighted bears, most too far away, but a few within good camera and telephoto range. Either black or brown (grizzly) bears, sometimes both, once lived everywhere that there were deer. Like the wild cats and wild dogs, the bears of North America

Rocky Mountain spring officially begins.

But the elk herds have always bounced back from winter's hardship. Except for whitetailed deer, wapiti are faring better than other antlered species. According to the Foundation for North American Big Game (see address in "Organizations"), the North American population had fallen to about 41,000 animals in 1907. Their survival was in doubt. Thanks in part to citizen concern and regulated hunting, but mostly to much better land management, the population in 1993 is about 740,000. The western wilderness would be empty without them.

Overleaf: *Roosevelt or Olympic elk during the rutting season. Bulls may acquire harems of as many as twenty cows.*
Overleaf left inset: *In the warm, sunny summertime, elk graze in harmony close together, or bed down during middays on the fringe of wildflower meadows.* **Overleaf right inset:** *Fighting head to head with antlers is a regular rite of every autumn, especially for younger elk bulls. Such sparring establishes rank and is good practice for the future.*

Left: *Bulls tune up for the rut and work off aggression by slashing at trees, shrubs, and then at one another with their antlers. A lot of foliage and turf can be torn up this way.*
Above: *One of the most exciting, most haunting sounds in the American outdoors is the shrill, calliope bugling of elk every fall. Bugling may be a challenge to other bulls, but far more likely it's a statement of availability to cows or the staking of a claim (to a harem). In any case, it's worth traveling far to see and hear.*

ROCKY MOUNTAIN ELK FOUNDATION

Unlike some other important animal species, the American elk has benefited from the formation and growing influence of a national guardian organization, the Rocky Mountain Elk Foundation (see address in "Organizations"). With both hunting and nonhunting members all across the United States and Canada, this nonprofit conservation group's main mission has been to raise funds for the direct benefit of elk and elk habitat, such as scientific studies and the purchase of land needed for winter range. Other wildlife has benefited as well. It is difficult to overestimate the importance of RMEF's contribution to the welfare of an animal revered by so many.

Above left: *A bull elk was closely guarding a cow (pictured), who was probably coming into estrus, and another rival intruded on the scene. The rival was soon chased away.* **Above:** *Young bulls sometimes snap off their antlers during their ritual sparring. These will grow back the next fall.* **Facing page top:** *A rare photo of strange elk behavior. Probably the female came into estrus late and is emphasizing that point to a very tired bull. But the behavior may have a different, unknown meaning.* **Facing page bottom:** *The rutting activities of elk every September in Yellowstone National Park usually take place near water, here along the Gibbon River, in open, grassy meadows. Bulls gather and defend their harems here. Either to cool off or to escape persistent males, the cows may stand in water for long periods. The bulls bugle in the early morning or late afternoon light. Altogether it is an exciting spectacle.*

Above: *Winter in Yellowstone National Park. Some elk spend the cold season in the vicinity of the Firehole River (pictured) and the famous geyser Old Faithful. Hot water might supply some warmth and melt snow to expose browse for the hungry animals.* **Right:** *It is November, and this elk herd is traveling across the Jackson Hole/Snake River valley. This is famous elk country, where some elk live year around. Others migrate a short distance south to spend the winters at the National Elk Refuge at Jackson Hole, Wyoming. This herd is moving toward the refuge.*

CARIBOU

In summer 1989, Peggy and I flew from Yellowknife, in Canada's central Northwest Territories, northward to Bathurst Inlet, where the Burnside River empties into Melville Sound of the Arctic Ocean. Our goal then was to photograph the musk oxen that spend the summer in that area and the migratory birds that nest in great numbers on the tundra. But we were distracted almost immediately. While exploring the cold inlet in a freighter canoe with Allen Kapolak, an Inuit guide, we suddenly were surrounded by a herd of caribou swimming from shore to Quadjuk or Backbone Island. Our main mission was immediately set aside, and our focus shifted to the caribou. We spent the next few days following the animals with cameras, traveling by canoe and also on foot.

We had intercepted one group of the Bathurst herd of Barren Ground caribou during one of two long migrations made every year. Altogether there are fourteen distinct caribou herds living in the vast tundra wilderness of northern Canada and Alaska. Each herd is pretty well confined to its own separate territory. Several of these territories are larger than the state of Ohio, but very few humans live in any of them. It is an inhospitable part of the world.

An Alaskan Barren Ground caribou bull in Denali National Park.

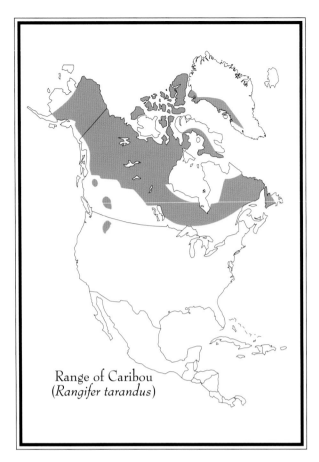

Range of Caribou
(*Rangifer tarandus*)

TO THE CALVING GROUNDS

No one can say exactly what triggered these Bathurst caribou we followed to begin their annual return trek that would last about eight months. All winter long they had endured intense cold, a meager food supply, and prowling wolves on their winter ranges far inland of the Arctic coast, in the headwaters country of the Coppermine, Burnside, and Yellowknife rivers. The Inuit call that wintering area the "land of little sticks" (known to us as taiga), for the short, sparse black spruce growing there.

But one day in March or April, an old female or probably several began slowly walking northeastward on old, familiar trails north toward Bathurst Inlet and beyond. All along the route, the paths of smaller groups joined, finally bringing together the entire Bathurst herd on their ages-old calving ground. There the calves that had been conceived the previous fall were born. When the new generation was strong enough to travel, the herd began its long return trip following the same routes. We met them as they were moving southwestward, crossing the barrier of Bathurst Inlet.

Nothing stopped or even detoured these caribou from their intended course. Not even the smallest calves hesitated to follow their mothers and plunge into water that had been firm ice only a few weeks earlier. On Quadjuk Island, all streamed after the lead animal over a steep and rocky spine that we could barely scale using handholds. This was the kind of place in which you would expect to find wild sheep or goats rather than wild deer. Having reached the other side of the island, the caribou once again had to swim the waters of Bathurst Inlet, this time for several miles more until they reached solid, dry ground.

We were waiting with cameras mounted on tripods near where they came ashore, and I could hardly believe how little notice they took of us. Some of the calves had a very difficult time climbing out of the water onto the slippery rocks. There also was a shaking off and sorting out period when the cows located the calves that had been separated from them during the swim. We could still see the animals at midnight, hoofing it into the distance toward the arctic sun when it dipped for a brief time beneath the horizon. In fact we watched the animals in the orange afterglow until the cool night wind died and hordes of mosquitoes attacked. Our only refuge was the canoe, paddled some distance from land. It occurred to me that the caribou had no refuge at all.

NORTH AMERICA'S TOUGHEST

Except for during midwinter, the Barren Ground caribou's life is one of constant movement, but the migration from wintering area to calving area is by far the most urgent and most difficult. Hundreds of miles must be covered. During this trek, weakened from winter's short rations, they must cross deep drifts and swim rivers choked with crumbling ice, all the while worried by wolves. Some days the wild winds never stop screaming. Still, this may be better than when the temperature suddenly falls far below zero Fahrenheit (-18° C), as it occasionally does, even in late spring. Strange as it may seem, heat can also be a problem. It causes rivers to swell and overflow. It turns snow into slush in the caribou's path. It can also bring on an early hatch of mosquitoes. In my opinion, the caribou are the toughest, the most tenacious of all the antlered species in North America.

Scientists generally agree that four subspecies of

caribou, *Rangifer tarandus,* inhabit northern regions of the New World, or Western Hemisphere. The animals we met at Bathurst belong to the race *R.t. groenlandicus,* of Greenland, Baffin Island, and the region northwest of Hudson Bay to the Arctic Ocean. *R.t. granti* is the race of interior Alaska and the northern Alaskan coast. *R.t. caribou,* the woodland caribou, lives in forests and subarctic regions completely across Canada. The white or Peary's caribou, *R.t. pearyi,* lives on Canada's northernmost islands in the Arctic Ocean.

Because of the regional differences in size and antler configuration, the caribou of North America have been divided into five (rather than four, the number of subspecies) categories by the Boone and Crockett Club for antler record-keeping purposes. These are mountain (British Columbia, Alberta, southern Yukon, and the Mackenzie Mountains, Northwest Territories); woodland (Canada from Newfoundland west to southern British Columbia); Barren Ground of Canada (Greenland and northern Canada); Barren Ground of Alaska; and Quebec-Labrador caribou. If all this is puzzling, still another subspecies, reindeer from Scandinavia, *R.t. tarandus,* have been released and are established on Nunivak Island and scattered areas in mainland Alaska.

Boone and Crockett records suggest that antler dimensions are longer on the average the farther west or northwest they are grown. Most of the super caribou racks have come from Alaska, with one most notable exception: In 1931, Zack Elbow obtained the largest caribou antlers of any subspecies or category ever measured—and by a good margin—in Labrador. It scored 474 points by the Boone and Crockett system.

SIZE

A full-grown Barren Ground bull will stand from three and one half to four feet (1.1–1.2 m) at the shoulder and weigh from three hundred to five hundred pounds (135–225 kg), depending on the locality. The long, flattened antlers, palmate on the ends, may stand three feet (0.9 m) high and have as many as forty points and two brow "shovels." Relative to body size (caribou are considerably smaller on the average than elk or moose of the same age), the antlers of prime bulls are the finest carried by any Cervidae. As mentioned

earlier, the cows of all caribou races, unlike any other Cervidae, also have antlers. These are much smaller than those of the males, however. The females shed their antlers annually, but later than the males do.

POPULATION

The populations of many arctic mammals—lemmings and foxes, for example—fluctuate greatly from year to year, and that of Barren Ground caribou does also. Biologists figure that the total population of all subspecies has averaged between one million and one and one-half million during the 1980s. Except for Alaska, the only caribou left in the United States are the twenty-five to thirty-five woodland caribou still clinging to existence in northern Idaho. There they are regarded as gravely endangered.

While today's caribou numbers may seem large, only a half-century ago the continental population was estimated to be three or four times as great. I have been visiting Denali National Park, Alaska, home of the McKinley herd, off and on since 1952. My trip diaries show that during that time the number of animals spotted has, year by year, gradually decreased. Standing high on Polychrome Pass one morning in 1955, I counted more than seven hundred cows, calves, and young bulls passing by on the deep, well-used trails far below. To see a herd of more than a dozen or so is very uncommon in the early 1990s.

MIGRATION

Over the millennia, caribou have evolved into skillful, unerring long-distance travelers. During migrations the group leaders, always older females, follow paths to the calving grounds that have offered the least resistance over time. The herd leaders seem to sense exactly which trails are hardest packed and safest. I have watched every animal in one group not only follow the leader's trail, but, moving in single file, step exactly in the hoofprints of the preceding animal. Moving this way conserves an immense amount of energy that would be lost if each made its separate way. On average a migrating herd covers about ten miles (16 km) a day, fifteen to twenty miles (24–32 km) if pressed by a late start, and up to forty miles (64 km) in extreme circumstances.

Most adult males do not join the springtime mass migration, although a few bulls might be seen among

We photographed this caribou migration at Bathurst Inlet, Northwest Territories. Here the animals, a cow and calf herd, are swimming across the Inlet (**top and center**) and swarming ashore. Some of the calves have difficulty getting a foothold (**bottom, facing page top**). As they continue, they cross a rocky island in mid-Inlet (**facing page bottom**), determined to continue the passage no matter what gets in the way, including a photographer.

the cow and calf herds. Instead most bulls linger in the wintering area until the melting winter snow-pack exposes more ground vegetation. They also move at what seems a more leisurely pace. In fact, the bulls don't really catch up with the females, who by this time are at or on their way to the rutting (wintering) grounds, until the green tundra turns a brilliant russet and crimson as the summer ends. All the while those splendid, majestic antlers are grow-ing. By the end of August in the far north, there are few more awesome scenes than those of prime bull caribou, moving across multicolored tundra, white manes and chest hair blowing in the wind. That view is all the more breathtaking if the antler velvet has just been shed, exposing cardinal red bone.

The shedding process occurs over several days, and soon after that the blood-red color of the antlers turns brown. The largest males are the first to lose their velvet, followed in order by progressively younger bulls. Often in Alaska's Denali National Park and Pre-serve, where the bulls grow massive racks, Peggy and I have photographed small bachelor herds with all antlers in dark brown velvet except for one set that was bright red. That pair invariably belonged to the largest of the males. A week to ten days later, all the velvet from all the antlers would litter the ground and flutter in the breeze. Interestingly, wolves in Denali have been seen eating the shed velvet.

MATING

When the days become cold and raw and the first snow flurries fall, the annual caribou rut begins. Smaller bands of cows join others to form large herds on the rutting grounds, which may be well within the northern limit of trees, or south of the treeline. All of the animals are fairly fat and sleek. Those older bulls, for example, have gained fifty pounds (22.5 kg) or more over the warmer months and thick lay-ers of white fat lay along their backs and rumps. All healthy males will have gained about 20 percent in body weight in just three months. The females have added about half that much. All of the North Ameri-can deer increase their body weight in preparation for the rut and winter, but no species as much as caribou.

If you are able to study a caribou gathering in the fall, you soon sense the tension building. The males especially grow more and more irritable and develop a rank odor. With increasing intolerance and rivalry the old buddy bachelor groups of summer break up. There is a constant seething in the herd as the bulls work out the order of dominance. The aura of estrus is heavy in the cold air. When the bulls can-not settle rank by pushing and posturing, violent fight-ing breaks out. From a distance an observer might see several antler-to-antler duels taking place at once. Caribou bulls probably resort more quickly to fight-ing than males of other North American deer, and their combat is more serious. Frequently bulls are killed or maimed to become easy prey for the always-following wolves.

Taking a closer look at a group, you may see a panting, hoarsely coughing bull following a cow that has come into estrus. Its neck and nose are extended as it approaches from behind to better detect the scents of the female. Often the sight of that one bull fol-lowing a cow will attract other bulls. If the original suitor does not intimidate the newcomers simply by turning his head to display huge antlers, a noisy battle takes place. In about two or three weeks, all of the cows will have been bred by a few of the best bulls, and the rattle of clashing antlers will slow and finally cease altogether. Now begins the season of the Hun-ger Moon, and it may be much harder on the breed-ers than on the bred.

Caribou males feed very little if at all during the active, turbulent rut. Already the fat reserves acquired during summer are depleted. Their antlers are cast away. But the cows retain their antlers longer and now use them to defend their calves and their own feeding areas from other cows and from bulls. In fact the females suddenly are dominant. Those fat, hand-some bulls of summer are reduced to aches and pains, skin and bones: the walking wounded. They are now as vulnerable to wolves as are the calves. Gradually the males regroup and reassemble in their bachelor herds that now have only second-class status.

EQUIPMENT

Winter in caribou country anywhere is a grim time that the unfit do not survive. To live until springtime, caribou depend on a remarkable body coat, their large hooves, and an unusual circulatory system. That body coat covers the entire animal so well that caribou never

Bulls of the woodland caribou remnant herd—gravely endangered—that still survives south of the Canada–U.S. border. The bulls are mature and have splendid antlers.

Above: *Caribou antlers are long, flattened, and palmate on the ends.*
Right: *A single bull with velvet just peeled from antlers and a bachelor herd, well camouflaged, travel toward traditional breeding areas in central Alaska.*

Above: Perhaps a victim of wolves, this bull, only its antlers and skull remaining, did not finish its annual migration to the breeding grounds. **Left:** In North America today, wolves survive in large numbers only in Canada and Alaska, although they have a small foothold in northern Minnesota and even smaller ones elsewhere in the contiguous United States. Wolves will kill moose, caribou, elk, or deer, the prey species depending on location and timing. Pictured is a six-and-one-half-month-old wolf, learning to hunt.

OF DEER AND WOLVES

Two or three centuries ago, the gray wolf (Canis lupus) was the most widely distributed mammal in the world. The species roamed widely across North America, Europe, and Asia, occupying many different kinds of habitats. The driest deserts, wettest rainforests, and loftiest alpine areas were the only places they did not inhabit. Wolves still survive across the Northern Hemisphere, but now only in the largest remaining blocks of wilderness that humans have not yet settled and "developed." More than half of their original range has been claimed by a civilization that seems determined to eliminate them.

In North America, the wolf is gone from Mexico. It also is nearly entirely gone from the densely populated strip across southern Canada, but is holding its own in the vast northern wilderness. In the United States a good population remains in Alaska, but politicians and developers there constantly think of new ways and new reasons to remove them. There are token numbers of gray wolves in northern Minnesota, Michigan's Isle Royale National Park in Lake Superior, and northwestern Montana.

Individual wolves are not as efficient predators of deer as are cougars. But wolves make up for it by hunting in families or packs and by their greater stamina. Adults average one hundred pounds (45 kg) or more over their range and vary in color from pure white to gray to brownish to almost pure black. The northernmost animals tend to be the heaviest and the lightest in color. That light pelage is a distinct advantage in arctic regions. All wolves, but especially those northern animals, have extremely dense underfur, which keeps them warm when winter temperatures fall far below zero.

Gregarious wolves live by a social code and structure that centers on (and is led by) a dominant male and female that achieve their rank by age, might, experience, and breeding. Pack bond seems strongest in winter when the hunting is most difficult and cooperation most necessary. Much of our knowledge of wolves comes from one biologist, L. David Mech. Mech has devoted most of his adult life to tracking wolves on foot and snowshoes, by boat and airplane, by telemetry and computer screen. His observations of the animals could fill a library.

Mech learned, for example, that despite a low success rate per hunt, wolves kill a lot of moose, caribou, elk, or deer, the prey species depending on location and timing. But almost nowhere did their hunting seriously threaten a deer population. These predators have lived in balance and harmony with their prey since the two evolved together. They might once again if humans would stop killing wolves at every opportunity.

shiver, even during the lowest temperatures that grip the Arctic. Body temperature is maintained with little or no increase in the metabolic rate.

A caribou's coat or robe is as effective an insulator as it is handsome. The brittle hairs are tapered on both ends, sealing moisture from the fine, thick wool beneath. This combination of outer, cellular guard hairs with dense underfur prevents warmth from escaping the caribou's body and maintains a body temperature of about 105 degrees Fahrenheit (41° C). Even a caribou's muzzle, except the nostrils, is fur-covered for protection when probing into snow for food.

Because caribou, especially the northernmost races, spend a significant part of their existence digging in snow for food, their large hooves have adapted especially for that purpose. An adult male's hoof measures about five inches (12.7 cm) square and changes shape to adapt to the northern seasons. The edges of the hooves are rounded off during the long summer migrations. But after the first permanent snowfall, the hard outer shell of each hoof develops a sharp edge and therefore a somewhat concave shape. This is perfect for breaking through ice crusts and pawing into packed snow. It also gives the animal better traction on slippery surfaces.

More unusual even than the hooves and hair coat is the counter-circulatory system in the caribou's legs. Similar to systems found in the flippers of northern seals and walruses, as well as in the legs of some birds, arteries running from the heart to the legs are located very near to veins running in the opposite direction. This allows an exchange of heat from warm blood to cold blood and helps maintain the temperature of the animal's legs at about 50 degrees Fahrenheit (10° C), well above freezing.

Altogether the caribou of the far north are extraordinary vagabonds. The magnificent antlers carried by the males of autumn are their crowning glory.

Above: *An Alaskan Barren Ground caribou bull in the magnificent Denali National Park in late summer. This is before the rut, with most of the bulls still retaining their antlers. Denali is the best place in North America to see such caribou trophy heads.* **Left:** *Woodland caribou bulls practicing some pre-rut sparring.* **Facing page:** *Shedding of the velvet occurs over several days. Soon after that, the blood-red color of the antlers turns brown.*

Above: *A late summer storm sweeps over the Alaskan tundra where a single bull pauses to browse.* **Right:** *A caribou's coat is an effective insulator, with hairs that block moisture and dense underfur.*

WHITETAILS

Let's assume you own the finest camera equipment money can buy. You have unlimited time to spare and can afford to travel anywhere. Your goal is to shoot pictures for a book such as this one of record (or near-record) antlers of each of the native deer. Which species would be the most difficult?

In my opinion it would be the most popular and abundant deer in North America or the world, the ubiquitous whitetail. Of course you could shoot plenty of photos of very good racks in almost every state and province. But focusing on one whitetail that qualifies for the Boone and Crockett record book recognition is another matter altogether. By comparison, moose, elk, caribou, and mule deer would be somewhat easier.

There are several good reasons for it. Although whitetails, *Odocoileus virginianus,* are the most abundant and widespread of all deer species, they are also the wariest of our antlered creatures. The older the bucks grow, the shyer they become, especially wherever open hunting seasons are held annually. Those super bucks do not reach their prime and maximum antler growth by being visible.

Early in my outdoor career, beginning in 1949, I worked for a few years as a game warden in Ohio's Division of Wildlife. At that time deer were beginning to recover from a low point in their population cycle. Deer sightings were not nearly as common as they are today, but were increasingly frequent. During the rut every fall we would find a few truly outstanding bucks killed along the highways in communities where no one believed that such bucks existed. The same animals that so easily escaped human detection throughout the year had not yet learned to cope with high-speed traffic on modern highways.

This Texas buck surely has some of the largest typical antlers ever photographed on a live animal. It scores about 190 points on the Boone and Crockett scale. The photo was shot in November during the rut, when the deer was about five and one-half years old, either at or near its peak of antler growth.

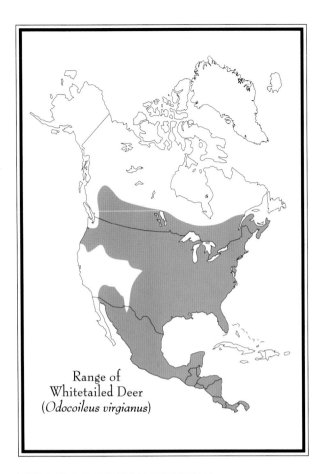

Range of
Whitetailed Deer
(*Odocoileus virgianus*)

THE GENTLE HERBIVORE?

The whitetail has been described as the gentle herbivore. Look at its handsome coat, its large brown eyes, its thin legs, and watch its graceful, even dainty demeanor. It is easy to understand why these animals seem frail and delicate, and why some regard them as too innocent to be hunted. But all these impressions certainly are false.

Thirty different races or subspecies of whitetails are distributed from Venezuela northward through nearly all of the United States to a deep band extending completely across southern Canada. The United States races gradually increase in body size from the Florida Keys deer, *O.v. clavium,* which is the smallest, moving northward to *O.v. dakotensis,* the northernmost and largest race. Outside a laboratory, all of the races are virtually indistinguishable, except in size, from all the others. Many deer biologists have even concluded that the deer have been mixed up so much by transshipment, restocking, and other deer management schemes that there is only one *Odocoileus virginianus* today. Period.

The fact that whitetails have survived the human onslaught of North America and now exist in what may be their greatest numbers ever is the first clue that they are not frail. Whitetails have survived the great climatic changes and have learned to live in more different kinds of habitat than any other native deer. These deer have also been exported to several countries in Europe, to Australia and New Zealand, and even to South Africa. However, in all of these alien places they are only a mixed blessing. They are in fact a good example of why it is unwise to introduce any wildlife into environments where they never lived and do not belong. Diseases are exported along with the deer, affecting valuable native species. Unchecked by natural predators, the foreign deer often overpopulate and overbrowse native vegetation. In some cases they can devastate long-established and delicate environments.

From a piglike ancestor, the "gentle herbivore" has evolved into a tough and swift creature able to run faster (on those thin legs) than any of their natural predators. They can travel as rapidly through dense second-growth evergreen forest as they can over prairies and rocky ground. They are also good swimmers. Watch a deer bounding away from danger across a snowy cornfield; it seems to be flying. All four feet seem off the ground most of the time.

Few animals have all their senses so keenly developed. A whitetail's eyesight is superb and especially quick to detect the slightest movement. Its sense of smell is good. But its sense of hearing may be the most acute of all.

Without looking up when feeding on acorns on the ground, a deer can differentiate a human footstep from that of a bear or a farm animal. It knows whether the movement of another animal nearby is fearful or calm. Sensitive ears that are tuned in all directions keep a deer constantly informed about what is happening all around. It is very difficult to approach a wild and healthy whitetail undetected.

PELAGE

The coat of a whitetail deer is another fine survival mechanism. From birth until the animal is about half-grown, its white-spotted reddish brown coat is surprisingly good camouflage, blending into a variety of habitats when the fawn is not yet able to outrun predators. During summers, adults sport a light reddish coat that is cool on hot days. At the onset of autumn this coat is shed and exchanged for a thicker one that holds heat far better.

Every winter we marvel at how efficiently the long guard hairs and short underfur insulate against subzero temperatures for weeks on end. Our Montana backyard whitetails can be covered with a layer of snow that does not melt and in fact acts as an extra layer of insulation. There is a cost in energy drain in changing coats twice each year, but apparently the resulting longtime survival, especially in areas where there is a great temperature variation, makes it worthwhile.

WHITETAIL COLOGNE

Each whitetail has four sets of external glands. The tarsal glands are marked by tufts of white hair inside the middle joints of the hind legs. These produce a scent that is unique to that particular deer, as human fingerprints are unique to the individual human. Metatarsal glands are located low on the backs of the legs, just above the hooves. Between the two hooves are the interdigital glands, which leave behind a scent trail as the animal wanders. Preorbital glands in the inner corners of the eyes act as tear glands. Altogether all of the glands are part of a deer communication system that also includes urinating. I once picked up a fawn whose mother had been killed by a car, and it urinated over both of us, which is typical behavior of fawns when frightened. Adults also urinate when they threaten or feel threatened by other deer. Aggressive whitetails and bucks in the rut rub their rear legs together and urinate on the tarsal glands.

TOOLS FOR SURVIVAL

Some deer are known by their vocalization—elk by their bugling, for example. Whitetails on the other hand are not very vocal. Some, but by no means all, bucks give a bleating sound when chasing does during the rut. Fawns may bleat when in trouble, but I have never heard a wild one make a sound. The noise most people do hear is a snort produced when the animal is surprised or ready to flush.

All deer have a keen sense of smell that may become even more acute during certain seasons. Smell identifies other deer, friends and foe, that may be approaching. It helps deer to find food, most of which

JAGUARS AND DEER

Historically the cougar was not the only large feline predator in North America. As recently as 1845, according to John Woodhouse Audubon, son of the pioneer bird painter, at least a few jaguars were living in Bexar County, Texas. Before that they ranged from southwestern Louisiana westward to southern Arizona, where the last one was seen north of the border in 1945. But the handsome spotted cats, which weigh from about 140 pounds (63 kg) (for females) to 250 pounds (113 kg) or so (for males) still live in scattered populations from Mexico to Brazil where they may kill some deer, including the whitetails that share their range, depending on their availability compared to other prey. To tell the truth, Panthera onca, *the jaguar, remains a predator no one really knows.*

is analyzed by scent before it is tasted. Some researchers believe that smell alone instinctively and instantly tells a deer if any vegetation is palatable and nutritious enough to be worth eating. Others believe it is more a combination of odor and taste. We do know that when whitetails approach a fall hayfield that has been half fertilized and half unfertilized, after smelling the field they will proceed directly to feed in the fertilized portion.

Not the least of a whitetail's escape-survival mechanisms are its two running gaits. If the need to get away is not especially urgent, the animal trots. It moves away with head and tail erect, the tail wagging from side to side. If the deer is really alarmed, it gallops, and this is a beautiful thing to watch, particularly where obstacles lie in the animal's path. The deer looks straight ahead, usually taking several long and powerful strides before making a long, high bound, easily clearing most things in its path. It then takes a few more racing steps before seeming to fly over the ground again. Over fairly open level ground, a deer can travel about thirty-five miles per hour (56 km/h), possibly a little faster. However, the entire

Top: *The end of the fall rut finds this fine, fat, ready Minnesota buck alert and with its neck still swollen. White-tails in the northern parts of their range must face months of a depleted food supply, which may be even more difficult to find under deep winter snows.* **Bottom:** *Whitetails live in various habitats across North America. This is riparian habitat along the Black River, Wisconsin.* **Right:** *A flooded cypress forest in north Florida where whitetails frequent the edges, sometimes grazing on aquatic vegetation. Deer swim very well here. This habitat is vastly different than that of whitetails elsewhere in North America.*

Whitetail fawns are left alone by their mothers for lengthy periods until the fawns are strong enough to follow them. It is a dangerous period of vulnerability to predators.

Surprised while feeding in a Texas oat field, a buck heads straight for the safety of dense brush.

whitetail physique and gait are best suited to escape in wooded country, as contrasted to the stotting—bouncing high on stiff legs while fleeing—of mule deer in more open range.

The antlers of whitetail bucks also are important to survival, although more indirectly. Large—usually the largest—antlers are important for successful courtship, which in turn leads to the finest bucks siring most of next spring's crop of fawns. I should mention here that recent evidence shows that powerful, heavy bodies may be as important as heavy racks in courtship success.

MATING

Prior to the annual fall rut (which is in November across most of the whitetail's range in Canada and the United States, later in the South), and after the shedding of antler velvet, a whitetail's neck swells to nearly twice its normal size, and its gonads become enlarged. Large bucks begin to rove, at intervals making scrapes on the ground with front hooves and urinating. On two occasions, in Ohio and Texas, I have seen bucks scrape also with their antlers. There are almost as many reasons offered for scraping as there are deer researchers, but most agree that to some extent it is a way to announce availability. Females also announce they are entering estrus by urinating near scrapes. When a buck discovers the alluring odor and the doe, he begins to follow her. Her aura will also attract others bucks. And inevitably, conflict.

Bucks begin random sparring as soon as the velvet sheds. For a while on Indian summer mornings, it is a tentative, almost friendly contest with the level of aggression very low. We have watched smaller subordinate bucks approach seniors and lick their foreheads as a prelude to a nonaggressive match of unequals. But as the daylight hours shorten, the tempo increases. There is no more lazy jousting between unequals. The really serious pushing and noisy antler clashes are between rivals of near-equal standing. Finally one backs down, the matter of status settled, at least between these two.

THE RUSH FOR ANTLER GOLD

One morning an elite squad of police stormed a seemingly abandoned, shuttered warehouse in a rundown suburb of Detroit. They had had many reports that dangerous drugs were being manufactured at the site. So the raid had been carefully planned and executed. But after searching the place and the occupants thoroughly, the officers found no trace whatever of illegal substances. What they did discover were shelves of whitetailed deer antlers— or rather of fake trophy whitetailed deer antlers— that two brothers were molding in plastic. Later, when placed side by side with genuine deer antlers, it was virtually impossible to tell the true bone from the perfect copies.

The intense search and the market demand for ever-larger deer antlers has taken some strange and unsavory turns. Law enforcement people have been kept busy trailing poachers. Taxidermy shops have been rifled, and antler "craftsmen" have tampered with real antlers, enlarging them. Nowadays, a set of record-book antlers can be worth its weight in gold.

This buck is wearing a maple leaf bough in its antlers after slashing at the tree in pre-rut sparring.

During my time as an Ohio game warden, I was called twice to try to separate large bucks whose antlers had become locked together. In one case one deer was already dead when I arrived, and after roping the live one to a tree (no simple job), I sawed off an antler of the dead one, thus releasing the survivor. I am certain it lived, but it may not have been well enough to participate in the rut that year.

In the other instance both deer were still full of fight, and it required the help of five strong young volunteers with ropes to subdue—hog-tie—the pair before we could use the saw. One of these bucks was ready to take on his human rescuers the minute he was free. Fortunately for us he thought better of it.

In both cases the ground all around was completely torn up from the violent struggles. In Michigan a hunter shot a buck that was carrying the head and antlers of another buck still entangled in its own rack. The weaker one had died from exhaustion, and in time, its head was twisted free from the torso. Game wardens later found its body, partially eaten by crows and a fox, laying on earth plowed up by the skirmish.

It is easy to write about and to emphasize the fighting of deer because it is exciting and dramatic, but far more often I have seen whitetails use their antlers for purposes other than combat. I have watched the use of antlers and foreheads for rubbing small trees, often completely ringing it of bark, thus dooming the tree. Most biologists say whitetails do this because the velvet on their antlers itches. Antlers come in handy for dislodging ticks and other insects from places the deer cannot reach any other way. One sunny day in Wisconsin we were entertained by a small buck that methodically snapped off all the branches of a rich, fall-red maple tree that it could reach with its antlers. The deer seemed to enjoy the destruction.

Winter in northern latitudes is the true survival test for whitetails, as it is for other creatures that share its environment. The frenzy and urgency of the rut tapers off. Each succeeding day becomes a little harder to endure as food supplies dwindle, energy drains away, and predators watch for their chances, which are now better than ever. Soon after the rut, bucks cast their antlers. Those in poorest physical condition shed their antlers first. That would seem to strip them of a major defense against predators when they need it most. But deer rely on sharp hooves, on swift legs, or some combination of the two, rather than on their antlers for defense.

In spring, even before the new generation of fawns is born, Peggy and I like to go hiking in the cottonwoods and spruce trees along Deep Creek, which hurries for a half-mile (0.8 km) through our property. At least a dozen whitetails always winter here. We explore to enjoy the new season's wildflowers and to gather morel mushrooms, but also to look for discarded whitetail antlers and other deer sign. One spring day we found the scattered skeleton and hair of one deer that had been killed, we are convinced, by the cougar that includes Deep Creek in its hunting territory. We also find scrapes and rubs from last fall's rut and antlers on which porcupines gnaw. Our whitetails are a treasure and pleasure the year around.

Facing page top: *Bucks begin random sparring as soon as the velvet sheds.* **Facing page bottom:** *Taking part in a rutting season ritual, this buck is marking his hoof scrapes on the ground and also rubbing and marking the tree branches directly above.* **Overleaf:** *Larger bucks lose some of their innate caution during the rut and are more likely to be seen than earlier or later in the year.*

Both photos: *Whitetail dueling during the rut can result in antler damage to a buck's eyes and ears as in the top photo. This deer is now blind in one eye. In the bottom photo, the bucks' antlers are locked together. Both animals are exhausted.*

The North American lynx and bobcat (shown) will prey on young deer and, during the most severe, snowy winters, on the most weakened adults. But their predatory role is small.

BOBCATS: POSSIBLE PREDATORS

Bobcats, which are widespread and relatively abundant all across the United States, and lynx, which roughly replace them across Canada, have some impact on deer numbers in North America. But both bobcats (Lynx rufus) and lynx (Lynx canadensis) are mainly hunters of much smaller game. The lynx, for instance, depends to a great extent on varying (also called snowshoe) hares year-round, so much so that its own population rises and falls with the periodic fluctuations in hare numbers. Nonetheless, neither bobcat nor lynx will ignore the chance to pounce on a fawn that is still too young to outrun them.

Bobcats are often accused of killing adult deer, and there are numerous records of them preying on the severely winter-weakened animals crowded into north-ern deer yards during brutal winters. I once found a healthy adult whitetail that had been half-eaten by a bobcat. At first I thought the cat might have been the predator, but later I determined from skid marks and tracks that the deer had been struck on the highway, limped off a short distance to die, and then was found by the bobcat, which was only a scavenger. Researchers in several states who have examined the contents of hundreds of bobcat stomachs have found venison in very few of them. One biologist, Ed Harger in Michigan, followed bobcat trails on foot for about 550 miles (885 km). During that time he found only four instances of deer predation. One kill was a young buck weighing about 120 pounds (54 kg). The other three were fawns.

Above: *This super, one-in-a-million whitetail buck, in its prime at five and one-half years old, was photographed on a northcentral Texas ranch during the rut. Such body size and antler growth are a result of a very sound deer management plan.* **Left:** *This buck has unusual antlers that grow almost straight up and with a rakish tilt to one side. It's a perfectly healthy animal.* **Facing page:** *The Columbian subspecies of whitetail is confined to a small area of coastal Washington. This buck, still in velvet and with still more antler growth possible before shedding the velvet, has unusually fine antlers.*

MULE DEER

Many of my most pleasant days have been spent hunting *Odocoileus hemionus,* the mule deer, with cameras. Fortunately Peggy and I have lived for a long time in Montana and Wyoming, where trophy muleys live in good numbers. And we're not far from Colorado, Utah, and Alberta, where mule deer bucks also carry heavy antlers every fall. Some of the trophies we've "shot" can be seen on these pages.

Not all of our hunts have been successful; in fact far too many have not. One afternoon on the steep Death Canyon trail in Grand Teton National Park stands out in my memory. Because it was drizzling, our cameras were sealed in waterproof plastic bags inside our backpacks rather than in our hands where they belonged. In autumn this trail is a very good one to encounter elk, which filter down from the high country toward the National Elk Refuge not far away. We seldom found many mule deer in this particular area.

A mile or so from the trailhead, the rain turned to sleet, and we paused to consider hiking back to our parked car. That's when Peggy noticed the buck standing on the slope above us and about sixty to seventy yards (54 – 63 m) away, warily watching us. It had extremely high and heavy antlers.

This fine, typical mule deer has made the trek from summer range high in the Alberta Rockies to the annual rendezvous with does at a lower elevation. A light snow covers the ground.

Fumbling now with five thumbs on each hand, I managed to retrieve the camera from my backpack. But before I could attach a longer telephoto lens, the buck was drifting away, still looking back at us. Too hastily I snapped a couple of pictures before the animal disappeared into a deep, dark draw. We never saw it again, despite returning to that same area during the next few days.

In our developed film the image of the deer was very small and slightly out of focus. But when projected onto a screen, the slides revealed what was, probably, the largest mule deer either of us had ever seen. The buck had eleven points, six on one side and five on the other. But the main beams and all the tines were very thick and seemed to reach two feet (0.6 m) or more above the forehead. We still compare all other mule deer we "shoot" with that Death Canyon buck.

RANGE

Mule deer range from Baja California and the Sierra Madre of northern Mexico to the northern borders of Alberta and British Columbia. The Pacific Coast region from central California north to Alaska is occupied by the closely related blacktailed deer. Some regard the blacktail as a subspecies of the mule deer, but other scientists insist the opposite is true. The ancestry of both can be traced to the Pleistocene era. Both evolved, along with the whitetail, from the same piglike Pleistocene predecessor.

A century ago naturalist-writer Ernest Thompson Seton estimated the continental mule deer population at about ten million before Europeans arrived in New England. But many modern biologists doubt it was even half that high. It is interesting that letters and journals of pioneers in the American West, as well as newspaper accounts of early western expansion, rarely mention mule deer. All describe instead the vast herds of bison, and to a lesser extent, the antelope, elk, and even the wild sheep a traveler might meet. It almost seems that mule deer didn't exist in numbers significant enough to impress anyone.

We do know that Native Americans of the West utilized many mule deer parts. The hides were sewn with sinew into leggings, dresses, capes, bedding, drumheads, and moccasins. Slivers of bone became needles. Although neither the meat nor the fat was regarded as highly as that of buffalo, no doubt it was never wasted. Consider also that Native Americans may have preferred the bison simply because they were easier to kill. From old yellowed sketches we see that mule deer antlers were used as ornamentation and as the tools to work flint into arrowheads.

SIZE AND APPEARANCE

Mule deer are named for their ears, which are much larger than those of their cousins, the whitetails. The size of the ears offers the best way to tell the two apart when only a front view is offered by the doe. The conformation of male antlers is also distinctive, differing from that of any other deer in the world. Whereas a whitetail buck's consist of opposing main beams from which other tines grow upward and inward, the main beams of mule deer and blacktailed deer branch into two beams and each of these into two again.

Generally speaking, mule deer antlers are larger than whitetail antlers. However, the size and quality of antlers is not the same in all parts of their great range. Certain areas where conditions for health and growth are ideal seem to produce the finest antlers year after year. Sometimes these areas are very small. As often as not they are deep wilderness tracts or sanctuaries where more males live long enough to attain maximum antler growth.

There are some western ranges where mule bucks attain great body weights, but some deficiency in nutrition or in heredity keeps them from growing antlers to match their size. The following are average weights of bucks taken in the northern Rocky Mountains and measured at hunter checking stations: yearlings, 125 to 130 pounds (56–58.5 kg) two-year olds, 170 to 175 pounds (76.5–79 kg); three- to five-year olds, 200 to 210 pounds (90–94.5 kg); six years and older, 250 pounds (112.5 kg).

Mule deer tend to be better, more approachable photographic subjects at any time of the year than any of the other native deer except moose. Some are extremely wary, but experience has shown me that on average muleys are as less suspicious of people than are whitetails or elk. That may explain at least in part why whitetails seem to be usurping more and more traditional mule deer range in the West. Some biologists fear that mule deer numbers are declining enough in several states to cause concern. Any photographer's best bet for finding trophy bucks is in the fall, preferably November in the northern Rockies, which is the rutting season.

MATING

Weatherwise, late fall is not always a pleasant time to be in the field. But it is that dramatic period when does are trekking downward from high summer ranges to congregate where early snows have not yet covered the ground. Estrus is triggered during the increasingly shorter and cooler days and is a magnet that seems to attract all the bucks in the vicinity. The rut activates scent glands on the hind legs and this also aids animals ready to breed to find one another.

Now for two or three weeks, any buck's antlers become its most valuable asset. It uses them to impress does and to intimidate rivals. The younger males, not yet really competitive in the breeding game, spar

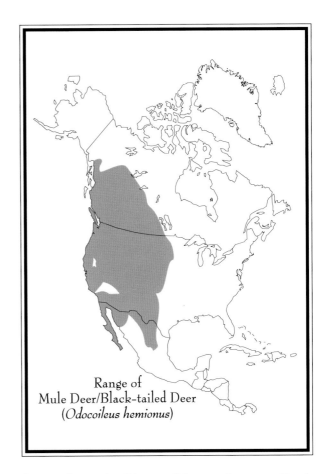

Range of
Mule Deer/Black-tailed Deer
(*Odocoileus hemionus*)

frequently on the fringes of the trysting areas. But it is uncommon to see larger males engaged in any vigorous combat. Large males of similar size certainly do fight, but usually only briefly, and it seems as a last resort. Studies to date show that just a few bucks do almost all of the breeding and that a sex ratio of one male to a dozen or so does is at least adequate, if not the best situation for successful breeding. In one closely monitored herd in Alberta, a single male impregnated seventeen does, which had twenty-eight fawns the following spring.

Mule deer does become sexually mature when one and one-half years old, or during their second autumn. Those that survive the first winter after the rut will bear fawns in late May or early June. The female's first pregnancy usually results in a single fawn. After that, twin fawns are not uncommon, and during some years in some areas, almost all of the does seem to have twins. Often fawn mortality is fairly high: Wolves, bears, wolverines, bobcats, even golden eagles take a certain toll on the very young animals.

But only rarely is predation an important factor in the size and prosperity of a deer herd. In fact pre-

Above: *Rainy Pass along the Pacific Coast Trail, Okanagon National Forest, Washington, is part of blacktailed deer country.* **Facing page:** *In the early autumn, a large mule deer buck emerges for a while from dark woods to feed on some fare that is less nutritious than what he found in summertime.*

dation may have a beneficial effect. Mule deer and the meat eaters have evolved together over the centuries, and most of the time the latter are culling the weakest, least-fit fawns from the herd. Habitat, particularly the quality of winter habitat, is much more a factor than predation in mule deer health and numbers.

What happens to male mule deer after the yearly rut is similar to what happens to other males in the deer family. They separate from the does to lead solitary lives or to join small bachelor bands. Breeding and competing have left even the most powerful and once-handsome bucks in poor or even emaciated condition. Very soon the antlers are cast. All bucks have lost a good bit of body weight. Now they are easier victims of predators than at any other time. Mountain lions especially take many of them. Winter is also the period when many are killed along busy western highways as the deer travel to lower elevations or try

to escape deep snows.

One winter I found a single antler near the carcass of a mule deer that had been struck by a speeding truck in Wyoming. I measured it and was slightly stunned. If that antler had still been attached to the skull, along with its opposite antler of equal size, it would have been the fifth largest mule deer rack in the record books.

Eleven subspecies of the mule deer, *Odocoileus hemionus,* are recognized. One, *O.h. cerrosensis,* lives only on a small island in the Gulf of California, another, *O.h. sheldoni,* only on an island in the Pacific Ocean off Baja California. Two others, subspecies known as blacktailed deer rather than mule deer, have larger ranges on the northwestern Pacific coast. *O.h. columbians,* the Columbian blacktail, ranges from California to British Columbia. *O.h. sitkensis,* the Sitka blacktail, lurks in the dense, evergreen coastal forest of southeastern Alaska.

112

BLACKTAILS

The life histories of blacktails are quite similar to those of the other muleys. Physical differences, easily detectable, are whitetail-like tails that are all black on the outside. The antler formation also is more like the whitetailed deer. Blacktails almost everywhere are more shy of humans and their activities than are mule deer. The bucks grow much smaller antlers: The largest blacktailed deer antlers ever measured would not even qualify for listing in the records among the typical mule deer heads.

We have had our share of interesting encounters with blacktails, though too few of them near enough for the best photography. Once when photographing seabirds on small satellite islets of Afognak Island, Alaska, we found a small Sitka buck swimming in the icy waters of Shelikof Strait. We followed it to a narrow beachhead where the animal splashed ashore and immediately disappeared into tall, moss-draped timber. That's the way it is, too often, with blacktailed deer.

Despite their shyness, their ability to disappear before your eyes, and their breeding prowess, blacktails seem to be on the decline. Clear-cutting the mature northwestern forests with such senseless speed, building roads on mountainsides that should be left untracked, and the sprawl of suburbia along the Pacific Coast are probably most responsible. While whitetailed deer are able to cope with expanding civilization, blacktails cannot do quite as well. Nor are they favorites of the timber companies because they sometimes eat newly planted seedlings, where the companies bother to plant them. Pointing a finger at deer is an attempt to deflect some of the public criticism of today's excessive timber-cutting practices.

Another interesting fact about all the mule and blacktailed deer (except those isolated on tiny islands) is that they share their range with at least one and usually several other members of the deer family as well as some horned big game. Within view of my Montana backdoor, for example, is a vast sweep of the Yellowstone River valley in one direction and the Absaroka-Beartooth Wilderness Area in the other. On

This portrait of a mule deer doe shows well the large ears that have given the species its name.

114

later Captain John Smith also found cougars in Virginia and wrote, "There be in this wilde lande lions, beares, woulves, foxes and muske cats [bob-cats]." Dutch settlers in Manhattan bought cougar pelts from Native Americans and mistakenly believed these were the same as African lions. Spanish colonizers in California and the Southwest became acquainted with cougars soon after settling in. But the sleek cat that once ranged from coast to coast and lived in every province and state (except Hawaii and probably Alaska) all the way southward to Tierra del Fuego, the tip of South America, now occupies only a small fraction of its original range. Cougars still live in modest numbers from British Columbia and Alberta through the western United States to northern Mexico. Here they haunt evergreen forests and snowy mountain meadows as well as the nearly waterless red canyons of Utah, West Texas, and Arizona. A relict population of fewer than fifty clings to existence in Florida.

Wherever they still live, cougars, or mountain lions, are important predators of (in order of importance) mule deer, whitetails, and elk. Experienced cats can kill animals much heavier than themselves. They are excellent stalkers and fast afoot. Like the other predators they have always been relentlessly hunted by humans, and are not really abundant anywhere.

MOUNTAIN LIONS: SLEEK PREDATORS

During a voyage to the New World a little more than five centuries ago, Christopher Columbus reported seeing a large "leon" along the Central American coast. This may have been the first sighting by a European of Felis concolor, the mountain lion (also called cougar, panther, painter, puma, or catamount). A century

Of all North American predators, none lives a more anonymous life than this one. The cougar is generally (except during mating) so silent and so agile on soft, padded paws that it can dissolve unseen into any environment. Our home place in Montana's Paradise Valley has been part of a local cougar's territory for several years, though we know of its presence only by footprints—once in snow past our front door—and by occasional deer kills we find along nearby Deep Creek. All of a cougar's senses, particularly eyesight, are well developed. "Our" cat probably sees a good bit of us, perhaps even from above, from trees that provide convenient horizontal limbs. Adults have powerful jaws with canine teeth one to one and one-half inches (2.5–3.8 cm) long.

Much of what we know today about cougars comes from a long and difficult study done by biologist Maurice Hornocker. During one project, which lasted for three full winters in the snowbound wilderness of northern Idaho, Hornocker and his assistant, Wilbur Wiles, trekked for hundreds of miles across rugged country in deep snow, practically living with mountain lions. The two men live-captured, tranquilized, tagged, and thoroughly examined forty-six different cats, many of them several times over, to learn how they lived. From those they fitted with radio collars, Hornocker and Wiles learned that males are solitary and so are females except when raising young.

Others of Hornocker's discoveries border on the astounding. While radio tracking one 105-pound (47-kg) female, which was still feeding two eighteen-month-old "kittens" as large as herself, the mother killed two six-point bull elk (among other game) to feed her family. Each of those elk weighed from six to seven times as much as the cougar. These kills illustrate more than killing ability alone. They tell us something about the prey as well.

Most members of the deer family are most vulnerable to predators when they are either very young or very old and infirm. Males, weakened and extremely vulnerable when the rut ends, are also at risk. The same strong, confident bull elk that has little to fear from a cougar in September is a more likely victim from January to April than the cows it impregnated during the autumn. Day in and day out in their western range, however, mule deer first and whitetails second provide most of the meat for cougars. Hornocker found that normally the "easiest" prey comprised most of a cougar's diet. In fact 75 percent of all elk and 62 percent of all deer captured by the cats in Idaho were either less than one and one-half years old or more than nine.

a winter day's hike in the latter, we might well find the discarded antlers of whitetailed deer, elk, and moose, as well as of mule deer. We have photographed blacktailed deer in Olympic National Park, Washington, not far from a small herd of mountain goats and with the bugling of Roosevelt elk faint in the background. Near Medicine Lake in Jasper National Park in Alberta one fall afternoon, we had caribou, elk, and mule deer in sight all at the same time. In Yellowstone Park, you are likely to encounter elk and moose almost anywhere you find muleys. More than once in high summer, when following bighorn sheep across high meadows and in precipitous, rocky places, I have been surprised to flush large mule bucks from their beds on the top of the world. It is not generally noted, but despite their somewhat awkward (compared to whitetailed deer) gait, mule deer are among the most sure-footed large creatures in the animal kingdom.

I like mule deer for many reasons, such as their accessibility and beauty. But maybe I appreciate them most of all because they have lured Peggy and me into many of the most beautiful places we have ever wandered, with and without cameras.

Above: *A mule deer buck tests the air for the scent of a doe in estrus.* **Left:** *This handsome mule buck, in October, has just shed all the velvet from its antlers and will soon begin the annual search and competition for does. Soon after this photo was taken, it joined other bachelors, tested the air for female scent (flehmen), drank in a mountain lake, and browsed on ripe chokecherries. It was joined briefly at water's edge by a spike buck.*

Facing page top: *This buck is busy in the pre-rut—slashing and dueling with saplings and brush, polishing antlers, marking, and scenting. The necks of all rutting bucks swell to almost twice the normal size.* Facing page bottom: *Fighting—sparring with antlers—is a fall ritual for mule deer bucks, especially younger ones, to determine rank in the breeding group. The largest males usually dominate by simply showing their antlers, not fighting.* Above: *These mule bucks are now active in the rutting competition, scenting (flehmen), trailing and tracking, and finally finding does that may be entering estrus. For a few weeks this is nonstop activity.* Right: *Studies to date show that just a few bucks do almost all of the breeding. This one may be tired of the "ordeal."*

Above: *Twin male blacktail fawns spend a summer together on the slopes of Olympic National Park, Washington, their spike antlers in velvet.* **Left:** *It is early winter, the rut all but ended; the first snows have fallen, and these mule deer bucks are prepared to make the best of the Hunger Moon. Their bodies are depleted of fat reserves, and they are now most susceptible to predators, especially cougars.* **Facing page:** *Now that the rut is over, the bucks are resting or searching for browse to regain lost weight. Does generally are in better condition to survive the deepening snow. Occasionally mule deer will "bunch up" in winter yards as here in northwest Wyoming.*

Above: *A blacktail buck still in velvet lurks in the lush, green, coastal forest of northwestern Washington.* **Right:** *This blacktail doe spends summer mornings knee-deep in lupine and other wildflowers of Hurricane Ridge, Olympic National Park, Washington.*

THE DEER OF EUROPE

During the Stone Age, a roster of remarkable large mammals roamed the brooding forests of the British Isles. Now most of these are gone. First to vanish was the giant elk, or giant deer, which may have become extinct in the British Isles well over ten thousand years ago. The animal was as its name suggests: giant. It stood six feet (1.8 m) tall at the shoulder, would have weighed well over one thousand pounds (450 kg), and had palmate antlers that spanned more than one hundred inches (254 cm). Displays of the massive antlers can be seen at the British Museum in London and in other museums in England. After these deer became extinct for an unknown reason, the brown bears, wolves, and reindeer disappeared. European Elk (called moose in North America) survived in the British Isles until the ninth century A.D.

Today the red deer is the largest animal still surviving in the British Isles.

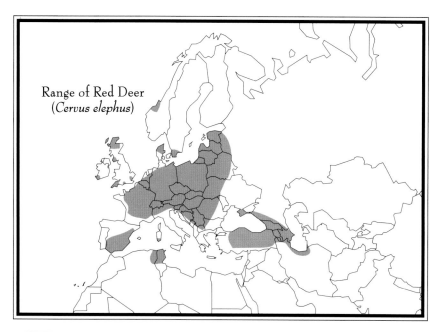

Range of Red Deer
(*Cervus elephus*)

late twentieth century in Turkey, Iran, and the southern USSR (now Russia), no one really knows the status of the deer known as the maral, *C.e. maral*. The fate of still another race, the hangul, *C.e. hanglu,* of Kashmir and Ladakh is in doubt because of the terrible religious conflicts and loss of central authority there.

Red deer are well named for the rich, reddish brown coat of summer that blends into gray for winter. Forest deer tend to be darker than those living in more open, sun-drenched habitat. All have yellowish brown rump patches. In some localities the deer have dark shading along the back. Calves are born white-spotted but lose the markings within a few weeks. I have also seen albino and cream-colored red deer in private deer parks. These probably are a result of selective breeding and inbreeding.

RED DEER

Today the red deer, *Cervus elephus scoticus,* is the only large Stone Age creature still surviving here. But rather than in forests, it now lives on cool, misty, treeless, heather slopes of the Scottish Highlands that humans find mostly inhospitable. Still this area offers by far the best chance for the long-term survival of this regal animal.

Elsewhere in its European and northern Asian range, the handsome red deer is living precariously on the edge. It still is the most widely distributed of all the Cervidae, largely because it has adapted to altered natural habitats. Now twelve subspecies of red deer roam in the mountainous, usually remote pockets from western Ireland eastward throughout Europe, into Asia Minor, Afghanistan, Iran, Tibet, and Kashmir to Chinese Turkestan, Siberia, and Mongolia. Some authorities even regard *Cervus elephus* and *Cervus canadensis,* the North American wapiti, as one and the same.

RANGE

A few individuals of a small subspecies no larger than an average mule deer, *C.e. corsicanus,* barely cling to existence on Corsica and Sardinia. A North African or Barbary subspecies, *C.e. barbarus,* found in a small coastal region on the Algeria-Tunisia border, is disappearing, and may already be gone. Following the revolutions, invasions, and civil disturbances of the

POPULATION

In 1960, two decades of very severe winters ended in England and Scotland with the red deer population at an all-time low. By 1990, it had rebounded to about three hundred thousand, according to the British Red Deer Commission. Most of these animals live and are intensively managed on fenced, privately owned hunting preserves. As with some deer species in the United States, these preserve deer owe their existence to the sport of trophy hunting. Commercial deer farms that raise the animals for meat are becoming increasingly important in many places as well.

MATING

Wherever they live, red deer are extraordinary survivors. Biologists point out that in the typical maritime climate of the Scottish Highlands, the grass and heather is nutritious for only about ninety days during normal times and for half that period during a very cold summer. The rut begins in mid-September, and it proceeds very much as that of the American elk. Stags compete vigorously and fight if necessary to become the master stags and to monopolize

A red deer calf hides in tall grass on a mountainside of South Island, New Zealand, where the species was introduced long ago.

RED DEER FAR FROM HOME

Some of the wild places where red deer still roam are almost halfway around the globe from Europe. To make new homes more like old ones, acclimatization societies and homesick expatriates have introduced red deer into Argentina, Chile, Texas, Australia, and New Zealand with either great success or tragedy, depending on how you regard it. The alien red deer have had an especially powerful impact on New Zealand. The first red deer reached there in 1851, and other small shipments arrived sporadically until 1914. Without any competition from any other grazing animals, and with no native predators, the deer population exploded to the point where serious, widespread, sometimes irreparable damage was done to the unique flora of the country. In some alpine regions, the vegetation was eaten down almost to bare ground.

Beginning in the 1970s, the New Zealand government began drastic action to reverse the damage to the environment. Unlimited sport hunting was encouraged. Helicopter crews captured thousands of animals alive for transfer to deer ranches and shot others for the meat. Once I joined a helicopter crew on a foray into the rugged South Island Alps to collect deer. We used expanding aerial nets, shot from guns during swooping, low-altitude pursuit of the terrified, stampeding beasts. That still ranks among the most hair-raising adventures of my life.

Red deer, for the record, were not the only members of the deer family to be released in New Zealand. Add also fallow deer from Europe; sambar, rusa, and sika deer from Asia; and elk, moose, and whitetails from North America. Some did not fare well. Others, like the red deer, would eventually become a problem.

the breeding of the hinds (females). One thing is greatly different though—throughout the rut, the stags advertise themselves with roaring that is lionlike and audible far across the highlands. This is in contrast to the shrill, calliopelike bugling of the American bull elk.

Among red deer, roaring contests often seem to be a better way to measure the strength of a rival or challenger stag than fighting with antlers. Only a few powerful males in the best condition can sustain the high rate and volume required to outroar all competitors. After close study, biologists in Scotland have concluded that roaring ability really is a measure of physical strength.

The antler conformation of mature stags also seems much different to me than those of Montana, Wyoming, and Alberta elk, which have taller, wider racks on the average. But the red deer racks tend to have more points. When viewed directly from the front, many red deer stags give the false impression of having multiple points growing upward directly out of the skull. We once photographed a stag with twenty points, ten per side.

The largest stags with the heaviest antlers are those of the race *C.e. hippelaphus* of central Europe. Great males weighing as much as six hundred pounds (270 kg) have been weighed in Poland, Bulgaria, Yugoslavia, Romania, and Hungary. That is almost twice as heavy as the largest Scottish stag.

Few obstacles except high fences can keep red stags away from hinds coming into estrus. Along the Scottish coast a dangerous strait with a powerful tidal surge separates two satellite islands of Jura and Islay. Nevertheless, every fall a number of stags swim between the two to reach females. Most probably make the trip safely each year—one way. But many, in a weakened condition, are known to drown on the return trip. On a game ranch in Texas, an eleven-year-old stag (with sixteen-point antlers) was known to have impregnated forty-seven hinds.

During the strenuous rut that may last more than a month, master stags are likely to lose a fifth of their body weight and as much vitality. They eat almost

Red deer hinds rest under a tree.

European (Scottish) red deer stag.

nothing during the search for romance. A recently majestic, aggressive animal may enter winter bedraggled, very thin, and even unsteady on its feet. Fortunately there are no predators to cope with, but until spring these stags must subsist mostly on sphagnum mosses and lichens. Preserve owners and gamekeepers may provide hay, potatoes, and mineral blocks for very large and valuable breeding stags. If living near the ocean, some red deer graze on seaweed.

A MATRIARCHY

Red deer herds are matriarchal. The groupings of hinds vary from twenty or so to as many as one hundred; the more open the environment, the larger the congregation. They spend most of every year traveling their territory, or heft, to take advantage of food availability, as well as of wind and weather conditions. Hinds leave the herds briefly in June to drop their calves in very nearly the same places that they themselves were born. More males than females are produced, but the ratio soon reverses because males

cannot endure harsh weather and illness as well as the females. A few Scottish stags have been known to reach thirteen or fourteen years of age. The healthiest hinds can live a little longer.

Males are not nearly as gregarious as females, although several may spend summers together in a sort of truce, traveling widely over their domain. According to veteran gamekeepers, stags tend to segregate themselves according to age or antler size. The young ones stay in their own loose groups, with the larger animals in usually smaller bachelor herds, always wandering. The very oldest that may be physically declining live solitary lives.

During August, when blizzards of insects may be very troublesome, males and females might briefly gather on the windiest, highest ridges to escape the torment. As many as eight hundred animals, young and old, of both sexes, might be seen together.

ROE DEER

Today a much smaller deer, *Capreolus capreolus,* the

132

The roe deer, this buck still in the velvet, ranges widely in scattered areas across the United Kingdom and Europe.

European roe deer, shares much of the red deer's habitat in Europe. Nowhere does it really exist in large numbers or on very large reserves. Instead small populations live in scattered, isolated habitat over much of Europe (except in Ireland) and in Asia Minor. To the east, in central Russia, is the very similar Siberian roe deer, *C.c. pygargus.*

In summertime, the European roe deer wears a rich, reddish coat not unlike the color of some red foxes. The red blends into gray on the face, and the species has a white chin. In winter

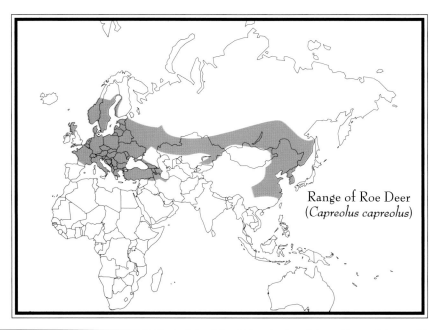

Range of Roe Deer
(*Capreolus capreolus*)

the bright coat turns to a gray tan with lighter flecks overall, and the rump becomes white. Newborn fawns, or kids, are rufous brown with light spots on the back and sides. I have not seen many roe deer in the wild, but I almost stepped on one very young fawn that was hiding in fairly short grass. The animal was so well camouflaged and remained so still that only the reflection in one bright eye caused me to stop short. It remained in place, probably with heart hammering, as I turned and walked away.

Next to the splendid racks of red deer, the mounted heads and skulls of roe deer are those most often found hanging in pubs and taverns, castles, homes, and trophy dens. Southern England and Scotland have produced fine roe deer heads, but antlers from Sweden average heavier. The largest roe deer antlers ever measured came from a buck shot in Hungary in 1965.

The main antler beams have six short points on each side. The new antlers are fully grown, and velvet is shed by early summer. The rut begins in late July or early August when it often is very hot in Europe, and the antlers are cast in October or November.

ELK

Scandinavia and a broad band of northern coniferous forest across Russia is the home of *Alces alces alces,* the European elk, or elch (known as "moose" in North America). In its outward appearance, diet, semiaquatic habitat preference, and general life history, it resembles

its New World cousin. Prime bulls may reach a half-ton (0.45 metric tons) in weight, but the palmate antlers, though very impressive, do not match the dimensions of those in Alaska and Canada's Yukon.

Especially in northern Scandinavia, elk are prospering because the forests are well managed and human impact on the land is light. In May or June most cows have single unspotted calves. Twins are considered common. In Sweden, triplet and, in one extraordinary instance, quadruplet calves have been reported. The elk population in Sweden was estimated at about 100,000 animals in the early 1990s.

Elk, particularly the bulls, are determined travelers. Several swam from Helsingfors Sound, in southwestern Sweden, ten miles (16 km) to Denmark where the species has been extinct for a thousand years. Periodic wars temporarily eliminated the species from the swamps and bog forests of eastern Poland, but newcomers from adjacent Russia are now completely protected.

Scientists have noted, without explanation, that the elk of Finland have two distinctly different antler formations. Those of northern and eastern Finland are palmated as elsewhere in the species's range. But the antlers of bulls of the southern and central areas usually are not.

REINDEER

Of all Eurasian deer, it is most difficult to write about the species that (thanks to Santa Claus) may be the

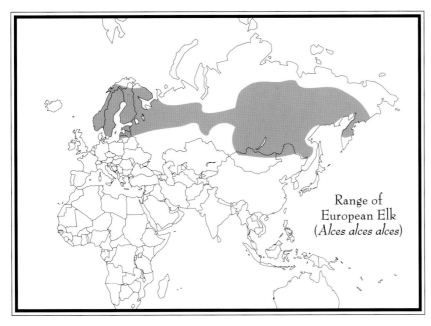

Range of
European Elk
(*Alces alces alces*)

hold, in the ninth century A.D. Limited small herds of wild reindeer occupy three reserves in Norway, although these may have been mixed with long-domesticated stock. The last wild reindeer in Finland was killed a century ago, but some may still live across the border in Russia. A small race of reindeer, *R.t. platyrhynchus,* lives in Spitzbergen, an island separated from Norway by 450 miles (724 km) of the Barents Sea. Nowadays the animals ranging across Scandinavia are considered *R.t. tarandus.* The reindeer of European Russia is classified as *R.t. fennicus.*

best-known deer in the world. There is no question but that the reindeer, *Rangifer tarandus,* survives in great numbers over much of northern Europe. But authorities are in sharp disagreement over the number (if more than one) of subspecies in existence, as well as over how many of the herds are truly wild. For example, it is believed that the last genuinely wild reindeer in Sweden was shot in 1865. The quarter-million animals still living in the country are herded, husbanded, and domesticated to various degrees by the Lapps.

Reindeer once lived throughout England and disappeared from Scotland, probably their last strong-

These have been introduced into Alaska as subsistence stock for native peoples, but at the very best are a mixed blessing. They are much more destructive to the fragile environment than native caribou because they do not migrate, and they must be tended by herders who are not especially diligent about husbanding the herds and watching for predators.

Some bull reindeer do grow impressive antlers similar in formation to those of caribou. But on the average, antlers are smaller and so is the average body size. The centuries of domestication seem to have drained a lot of vitality from a once splendid wild species.

Range of Reindeer
(*Rangifer tarandus*)

FALLOW DEER

Originally introduced into Europe from Asia Minor about two thousand years ago, the fallow deer, *Dama dama*, still roams in scattered woodlands, but for the most part lives in fenced parklands and estates across the European continent. They are also well established in several locations in the United States.

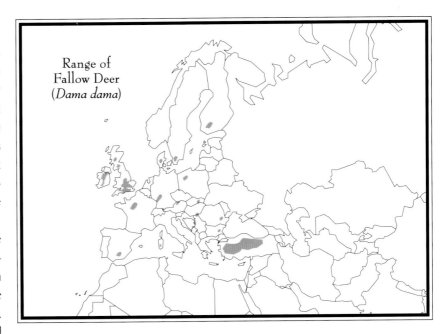

Range of
Fallow Deer
(*Dama dama*)

What is often regarded as the typical fallow deer is a fawn-colored (in summer) animal with white spots that usually become gray or mouse-colored in winter. However none of the world's wild mammals exhibit more color variations than this one. We have seen and photographed herds of all white and all black fallow deer. Also there are brown, brown-spotted, pinto, and silver-blue individuals that have resulted from centuries of selective breeding in game parks and collections.

When living on good range or provided with ample nutrition, mature fallow bucks grow impressive, even massive palmate antlers for their modest body size. In conformation, these antlers fall somewhere between those of a mule deer and a small bull moose.

The fallow rut in both Europe and North America begins in early October and males are extremely vocal. We have heard their rolling grunts from at least a quarter-mile (0.4 km) away. But more noteworthy than the grunting is the unique rutting ritual, called lekking. *Lek* is a Swedish word that translates roughly into a frozen area—or arena—for sports or contests. Zoologists have long used the term to describe a traditional mating area where males establish and defend territories toward which females congregate when they come into estrus.

Lekking is the common breeding pattern for several African antelopes and for some birds, such as the North American sage grouse and European black grouse. But fallow deer are the only members of Cervidae to use leks. At least one fallow herd in Europe has been using the same lek for at least 160 years.

In 1828 the English artist J. M. W. Turner painted a landscape of Petworth Park in Sussex, England. In the center of the painting two fallow bucks are sparring in the pale October sunlight among oak trees while other males watch from stations all around. Elsewhere, herds of does graze peacefully. Recently biologist Tim Clutton-Brock visited Petworth and found a scene astonishingly similar to that in the painting. As a result he went on to study why fallow bucks defend the very small territories of a lek rather than actively pursue females each fall, or gather harems as do some other deer. After five seasons of careful observations, he is still searching for the answer.

Facing page top: *Young white fallow bucks spar, probably as a training exercise.* **Facing page bottom left:** *This photo illustrates the unique conformations of antlers in large fallow bucks. The antlers more resemble those of moose than of other deer.* **Facing page bottom right:** *Chital or spotted deer from India have been introduced and roam over many European game parks, where they add bright color. They also have been established and are living in widely scattered areas in the United States.*

CONSERVATION AND THE FUTURE

During October 1993, two large bull elk were killed in Wyoming's Yellowstone National Park during the rut, when the animals are most vulnerable. Photographers have found elk carcasses left to rot, the antlers removed, and the culprits remain at large. Late one winter night, a poacher drowned while trying to secretly float a rubber raft full of antlers out of the park via the Yellowstone River.

While working on our book *Whitetails*, Peggy and I learned about antler poachers elsewhere, in fact about rings of antler poachers, that were then getting away with super deer antlers on ranches in southern and West Texas. In one well publicized case, nine West Texans were finally caught shooting large whitetailed bucks from a helicopter. No one knows exactly how many trophy antlers they got altogether. The chopper, valued at seventy-five thousand dollars, was confiscated, but otherwise the poachers were not greatly inconvenienced. In some Texas counties known for producing trophy whitetails, poaching by individuals and small groups can resemble small-scale guerrilla operations.

Poaching is a terrible problem wherever trophy deer exist. This fine bull elk, here in its velvet, disappeared from Yellowstone National Park soon after the velvet was shed. The odds are high that it was killed by poachers.

ONE POACHER'S TRACKS

Early in 1991, outdoor photographer Scott Carpenter noticed photos in a national magazine of one Donald E. Lewis posed with a trophy mule deer with a massive rack of antlers that he had shot. The captions said the pictures (and the deer) were taken in Montana, but Carpenter thought the terrain looked much more like the red sandstone country near Kanab, Utah, where he lived. That area is known for producing trophy mule bucks. Later, by remarkable coincidence, Carpenter and his friend, Ryan Hatch, another photographer, ran into Lewis in southern Utah.

They also began to find abandoned, recently killed deer carcasses, all with the antlers separated from the skull in the same ritualistic way. The cameramen put two and two together and decided to shadow Lewis. Ryan Hatch even followed him on a hunting foray into Arizona.

In November, Utah state game wardens noticed a suspicious pickup truck parked just outside Zion National Park. Nearby they had found more deer carcasses with the antlers missing. When the officers arrested Lewis, trying to drive away, they found fresh deer antlers in the vehicle that Lewis claimed he had just taken legally in Arizona not far to the south. (Later, photographer Hatch was able to testify that Lewis did not take any deer in Arizona.) But far more important than the antlers were six videotapes and handwritten notes also found in the pickup. They revealed that for at least ten years Lewis had been on a criminal binge, taking trophy antlers by any means whatever in several Rocky Mountain states. The story of that spree, which came to light after many months and hundreds of hours of investigation by state and federal law enforcement personnel, is as sobering as it is hard to believe.

In 1991, Lewis, a thirty-nine-year-old native of Alabama, admitted to investigators that he was only building his image as the world's greatest trophy bowhunter. In this he had been very successful. Because of his notoriety, by 1990 he was on the publicity payrolls of companies that manufactured firearms, archery gear, clothing, game calls, and arrows. One archery magazine featured him as "Mr. Big Bucks," who had already killed twenty-two record book mule deer. He was featured in hunting equipment catalogs. Lewis claimed to have taken record mule deer antlers in each of three states, Montana, Wyoming, and Idaho, two years in a row.

Investigations after his arrest punched some holes in most of these claims. A search of the records showed that he had not bought hunting licenses in some of these states where he had reported success. Rifles instead of bows and arrows had been used for some of the bowhunting "records." Lewis had planned to shoot an Alaskan moose and then haul it to Wyoming where he could claim it was an enormous Shiras moose, a subspecies genetically smaller than the Alaskan moose. Most, if not all, of the large elk he shot were taken in Yellowstone National Park, where hunting has been

In reality almost no area where antlered animals live is immune to this kind of activity. During the mid-1980s, Peggy and I spent a cold but exciting winter afternoon photographing an outstanding bull moose in Grand Teton National Park, Wyoming. It browsed almost within sight of the Jackson Lake Lodge. The animal was well known locally, and other camera people were also on that scene exposing large amounts of film. At dusk we drove homeward toward Teton Village, and along a narrow back road within national park boundaries, we spotted a bull elk every bit as impressive as the moose we had just left. It was standing silhouetted on a low ridge just above the road. We marked the exact location and planned to return the next morning when there would be sufficient light for photography.

We need not have bothered. Soon after daybreak we returned, but there was no bull elk. Instead we found the bloody ground where it had been shot during the night and dragged down the slope to where a truck probably waited on the road. Lack of funds for adequate patrolling and law enforcement had made this a common occurrence in Grand Teton Park.

There is more to this story. The next year that

illegal for a century. Lewis began his poaching career there in 1983 and poached every fall until 1991.

For decades each September, photographers and enthusiastic wildlife watchers have converged on Yellowstone Park to witness the annual elk rut. Here majestic bulls that had little fear of humans strutted and bugled in open meadows to compete for harems of cows on glorious, bright mornings. It is—or was—one of the great wildlife spectacles in North America. One area where the elk watching was always particularly good was along Indian Creek in the vicinity of a public campground that was closed by the time the rut began. For several years I had noticed, and fellow wildlife photographers had agreed, that the elk of Indian Creek had become increasingly shy, and by 1991, bulls were seldom seen there at all. It is now almost impossible to approach any elk in that vicinity.

And no wonder: Don Lewis had been hunting there, just out of sight of both the public and park game rangers for nine years. He had started even while Operation Trophykill, a three-year undercover poaching investigation in the Yellowstone area, was underway. (Incidentally, at its conclusion Trophykill brought fifty poachers to justice. They were fined a combined $128,138 in 1984 and served a total of fifty-one years in prison.)

One of the incriminating videotapes found by Utah wardens in Lewis's pickup shows Lewis and Arthur Sims, also of Alabama, shooting thirteen elk with bows and arrows near Indian Creek Campground, some

from as close as twenty feet (6.1 m). Nine of the elk died. One is shown staggering away with arrows sticking out of its intestines. None of the elk meat was retrieved. The largest antlers were packed out after dark and shipped to Alabama. Lewis and Sims had planned to market the video as a commercial on how to hunt trophy elk.

The aftermath of this case is almost as sickening as the deed. Neither Sims nor Lewis ever had to stand trial. They plea-bargained, by mail, to misdemeanors, and each paid fines of $15,000 for poaching elk in a national park on just one occasion. Lewis did have to serve jail time in Utah for poaching the mule deer there. Nobody knows exactly how many fine antlered animals he and his friends killed in New Mexico and Colorado, as well as the states already mentioned. Feature writer Michael Milstein of the Billings (Montana) Gazette *had to resort to the Freedom of Information Act to obtain material for his investigative article that exposed these crimes in his newspaper. The chief federal prosecutor in the case, Richard Stacy, didn't believe a "wildlife crime" rated a more serious penalty. He did not prosecute Lewis at all for interstate shipment of illegal wildlife, which is a felony under the federal Lacey Act.*

It would be gratifying to think that with Don Lewis out of the antler business, poaching is finished. Of course it isn't, and as Operation Trophykill showed, he wasn't the first to violate game laws.

same bull moose we had photographed reappeared in the same area near Jackson Lake Lodge, this year with even heavier antlers. Perhaps thousands of visitors watched it almost daily. The moose paid little attention to people approaching it with cameras. Then in late fall, when the park had emptied of summer visitors, an archer shot the moose, removed the antlers, and vanished in the night, leaving the carcass behind.

Law enforcement officials, overextended almost everywhere, admit that 90 percent or more of poachers are never caught. But in this case the killer made two mistakes. First, he removed his engraved watch

and hung it on a bush while freeing the antlers and forgot to retrieve it when he hurried away. Rangers found it on the site. Later, he entered the antlers in the Pope and Young Club's annual competition. That was mistake number two. He was immediately trapped. Hundreds of photos of the bull moose alive in a national park had been taken and they matched exactly the rack in the contest.

Law enforcement officials are convinced that poaching various species in the Rocky Mountain region of Canada and the United States alone is a business worth more than a billion dollars a year. A

lot of that comes from the sale of bear gall bladders and velvet-covered elk antlers to dealers in the Far East. There is also a seller's market for trophy bighorn sheep heads and other horns. The rest is made from the sale of trophy antlers. A German hunter paid twenty-five thousand dollars in cash for an elk rack that investigators believe was shot in Jasper National Park, Alberta. A number of the magnificent bull elk that long lived within a few miles of Jasper townsite have mysteriously vanished.

In 1992, depending on measurements and general attractiveness, poached elk racks were selling for from five thousand to twelve thousand dollars. Record-book whitetailed deer heads, probably the most coveted of antlers in North America, were going for from twenty-five thousand to fifty thousand dollars. (The source for these figures is the U.S. Fish and Wildlife Service and Montana's Department of Fish, Wildlife and Parks.)

But as terrible as it is, the tremendous toll poaching takes on wildlife is not the most serious limiting factor to producing a large, healthy crop of antlered animals every year. The bottom line—what *really* counts—is the quality of America's and the world's environment.

There are a number of important steps we absolutely must take soon to save our large animals, as well as the butterflies and beetles, the squirrels, woodpeckers, porcupines and everything else that shares the land with them. First, we need to strictly preserve, totally undeveloped, all of the wilderness that still remains anywhere. That includes wetlands and prairies as well as the forested mountains of the West. We must reexamine the grazing laws for public lands, and on almost all of these, reduce the amount of livestock grazing while increasing the fees paid for its use. Applying pesticides and using poisons for predators on public lands must be stopped. Timber cutting policies for our national forests must be reviewed, and the rate of cutting drastically reduced.

Consider one example in Montana where, for a long time, environmentalists have warned that timber companies were cutting trees far faster than they could possibly grow back. Two of the largest lumbering companies, Champion International and Plum Creek, denied it and used their considerable political influence to stop passage of any laws or regulations that would slow them down even slightly. Now vast areas of northwestern Montana lie clear cut, ugly, and eroding. Champion closed its mills, laid off workers, and is cutting and running. The company's legacy in a once green, wooded watershed is total disaster.

Sadly, that is the same scenario from California northwestward to Alaska. Nowadays we think of the tropical rainforests of Brazil and southeastern Asia as being the most despoiled on earth. But I have never seen forests more completely, brutally cut than they have been in British Columbia and parts of southeastern Alaska.

TOO MUCH OF A GOOD THING

Elsewhere the problem is vastly different. In parts of the eastern United States one of wildlife management's greatest success stories has suddenly turned sour. Early in the twentieth century, whitetailed deer numbers were very low in the eastern United States, and programs were instituted in every state from Georgia to Maine to increase the herds for hunting. Now in the early 1990s, deer exist in record numbers, perhaps to five times as many per undeveloped acre of land as when settlers arrived from Europe. Now we have such an overabundance in some places that the deer are inhibiting forest growth and reducing the diversity of many plant and animals species. Agricultural damage is heavy. The deer are also an expensive nuisance in many suburban areas.

But this problem can be corrected, and fairly quickly. What we need are longer, more liberal deer hunting seasons, which reduce the population to the carrying capacity of the land. Most biologists agree that such a reduction will also gradually increase the average antler size by providing more and better nutrition for each deer.

Antlers, like the health and numbers of the animals that carry them, are an unfailing index of the quality of the land. *Our* land.

Antler poachers working in Yellowstone were frightened away by rangers after removing only one antler of this bull. The carcass was left to rot.

Above: *One key to good populations of members of the deer family, as well as good antler growth in males, is a pure environment that furnishes food and cover the year around.* **Facing page:** *Wildfires like this massive blaze in Yellowstone in 1988 can greatly change the environment, both for better and worse. First it may destroy badly needed winter range for the antlered animals—and many may starve as they did in Yellowstone. But in time fresh regrowth more than makes up for it.*

"GOOD GUY"

Every fall a good many men risk their lives in the pursuit of poachers. Typical of them is Roy Burke of Montana's Fish, Wildlife and Parks Department. With its wealth of big game and wilderness, Montana is a magnet for poachers. To try to catch them Burke has spent a lot of time in saloons and other dark places, posing as a guide on the take, a businessman looking for a deal, an out-of-state sportsman, or even a renegade wildlife warden. To hide his identity, he has grown numerous beards, dyed his hair, and tried to change his western accent. As a result he admits he has seen about everything in the way of poaching and illegal wildlife dealing. One night he was attacked by six young men, all seemingly high on drugs, who he feared had identified him. But not quite—they thought he was a narcotics agent. They were going to kill him, but somehow he talked his way out of it. Nowadays some poachers are also dealing drugs during the off-season.

An antler shed by a bull moose. If the animal survives winter and finds adequate nutrition during the next summer, it will discard an even larger antler late in fall.

TAKING TROPHY PHOTOGRAPHS OF ANTLERED ANIMALS

Most of the pictures in this book were taken on land that is open to the public, specifically in national wildlife refuges, national parks and forests, and state parks where there is little or no hunting. It is extremely difficult, sometimes impossible, to approach any antlered animals within reasonable camera range where hunting takes place. The only exceptions to the above are some of the whitetail photos that were taken on private preserves where big bucks are a specialty.

Altogether the photos represent about twenty years in the field and the exposure, roughly, of from twelve hundred to fifteen hundred rolls of film. We have photographed antlers in fair weather and foul, in heat and numbing cold, by car and canoe, on snowshoes and cross-country skis, by climbing and wading, but mostly by alternately hiking and playing the waiting game. On a number of occasions, we (or an accomplice) have called animals into closer range by rattling antlers, grunting, bugling, or by using scent. Murry Burnham of Marble Falls, Texas, has been our invaluable mentor in successful game calling and rattling. Be aware that baiting, rattling, or the use of any attractants whatsoever is strictly forbidden in national parks.

A super whitetail trophy deer — as well as a trophy photograph.

CAMERAS AND FILM

All of our images were taken with 35mm single lens reflex (SLR) cameras equipped with motor drives. Perhaps half (the older ones) were taken with manual focus lenses, the rest with autofocus. We have employed a variety of lenses: a 35–80mm zoom mostly for the landscapes; 80–200mm zoom for certain scenes and for the least shy animals; 300mm, 400mm, and 600mm telephoto lenses for most of the animal subjects. With the latter three telephotos we also used tripods sturdy enough to comfortably support their weight. Instead of the monoball tripod heads, long regarded as the best for wildlife photography, we recently switched to a Wimberley head (see address in "Organizations"), which is vastly superior when moving, wary wild creatures are the subjects.

We have used and still use all of the positive or slide films on the market over the past twenty years: fast, medium, and slow speeds. Despite advertising claims and countless test reports, not one of them is best for every situation, or even for most wildlife and nature photo opportunities. So when seriously shooting, we shoot several different kinds of film.

Peggy and I work close together all the time, but shoot from slightly different angles, distances, and viewpoints. There are many advantages to this, not the least of which is rich companionship. For a long time we have not been able to tell who took which photo and waste no time trying to do so.

VEHICLES

In wildlife photography anywhere for any species, other equipment is just as important as the camera gear. We travel in a light van that is a "hunting" camp wherever we park it. It has a collapsible bed, small refrigerator, propane stove, and storage compartments, yet is roomy enough for too much photo equipment. By being able to overnight near or among our subjects, we can easily be set up before daybreak, ready to catch the early, best light of day. It also allows us to linger in the evening for the last, low rays of sunlight that just might illuminate our subject in a golden glow.

When on the road we have found no better choice of campgrounds than those of KOA, Kampgrounds of America. Their high standards ensure the camper of secure, clean, attractive surroundings plus the luxury of a hot shower. A directory of their campgrounds is available for $3.00 (see address in "Organizations").

CLOTHING

It's hard to overemphasize the importance of proper clothing and footwear—you'll never be able to concentrate on your subject if you're shivering from the cold. We keep the best and warmest hanging handy in our van: pants, cap, gloves and jacket by Sleeping Indian Designs (see address in "Organizations").

It is difficult to beat Sleeping Indian clothing when shooting in subzero temperatures. Both the pants and jackets have plenty of secure pockets to hold film and filters plus tissues, car keys, and any other small items needed. For extra lenses and larger things, Sleeping Indian makes a matching rucksack. The fabric is two-ply, worsted wool that is warm, tough, supple, comfortable, and quiet in the field (unlike most synthetic materials that rustle and gleam). Wool resists water, but is warm even when wet. We can sit or even lie down in the snow to shoot low angle photos without chilling. The soft-edged camouflage pattern blends into the background and offers some concealment. The gray-to-white color blend works well in a snowy landscape, the brown-tan combination is best in bare, weedy country. Wildlife photography in the dead of winter had never been a very pleasant activity, but Sleeping Indian gear has changed that. Especially noteworthy are their three-layer gloves for more deft camera handling.

Some other valuable equipment items we have needed are backpacks, beltpacks, a lightweight photo vest, calls, and blinds. By far the best blind is the Rue Enterprises' Ultimate (see address in "Organizations"), which is roomy, quick to set up, and at only nine pounds (4 kg), very portable. We have also put the Rue Pocket Blind to very good use. This is simply a closed-top cylinder of camouflage cloth with ports for eyes, hands, and camera that slips over both photographer and camera. Whether you're sitting, crouching, or standing, you're covered from head to toe. Rain hoods (or an umbrella) for cameras and lenses, especially in rainy places like Alaska, are valuable, and are also available in the Rue catalog.

There have been times and places each year when one photo accessory has been more vital than all the rest: insect repellent. In summer we never leave home without it.

Scenes of antler country in Montana. Mule and whitetailed deer, elk, and moose live here.

Murry Burnham rattles antlers as Peggy Bauer waits to shoot photographs of an approaching buck.

TROPHY HUNTING WITH A CAMERA

Admittedly, what makes a true trophy head of any species may be strictly in the eye of the beholder, a fact that lures more and more outdoorspeople to go trophy hunting with a camera or simply for the enriching experience of seeing a fine male deer specimen during a haunting, golden autumn when the natural world is at its most spectacular.

Antler watching and photography are challenging and rewarding pastimes that are possible from some suburban backyards to the deepest wilderness. You can work at these hobbies as hard or as leisurely as you like. There are no closed seasons or bag limits and no licenses to buy. Following are a few guidelines for finding and identifying large or larger-than-average antlers.

First, search in a suitable habitat. For example, you are not likely to find elk or mule deer sheds in any numbers or of large size in badly over-grazed, over-utilized lands in the western United States or Canada where the nutrition is poor. The odds for success increase when you concentrate on wintering areas of na-

tional parks and reserves and on national and state wildlife refuges where gun hunting is not permitted. Animals used to the security of protected lands grow less leery of people with field glasses and photo gear. Keep in mind that you may not collect discarded antlers in national parks and some other sanctuaries.

Definitely recognizing a trophy head in the field is not easy. A bull or buck does not reach ripe old age and maximum antler size by being unwary and rarely will it linger long enough for a careful study. If at all possible, try to get a good look at the antlers first from the front and then from the side. Forget body size and anything else distracting. Concentrate on the antlers. Elsewhere in this book I've described what constitutes what might be considered trophy size for each species of Cervidae. Studying the photographs in this book also should be helpful.

For many years now Peggy and I have been evaluating and recording antlers through the telephoto lenses of our cameras. Fortunately, we have seen and squeezed the shutter on our share of super specimens. In all the world there is no sport to exactly match it.

Left: Peggy Bauer uses a 35mm single lens reflex (SLR) camera and zoom lens to photo bull elk bedded in Yellowstone National Park. **Facing page:** A most compact and portable—and our favorite—field blind is the L.L. Rue Ultimate, shown here in use.

A very large elk, bugling in September.

ORGANIZATIONS

BOONE AND CROCKETT
CLUB
Old Milwaukee Depot
250 Station Drive
Missoula, MT 59801

BUCKHORN HALL OF HORNS
Lone Star Brewery
600 Lone Star Boulevard
San Antonio, TX 78204
210-270-9465

FOUNDATION FOR NORTH
AMERICAN BIG GAME
Box 2710
Woodbridge, VA 22192

KOA, KAMPGROUNDS OF
AMERICA, Dave Nusbaum
P.O. Box 30162
Billings, MT 59107
406-248-7444

LONGHUNTER SOCIETY
P.O. Box 67
Friendship, IN 47021

NORTH AMERICAN SHED
HUNTERS CLUB
19790 Dogwood Street NW
Cedar, MN 55011

POPE AND YOUNG CLUB
P.O. Box 548
Chatfield, MN 55923

ROCKY MOUNTAIN ELK
FOUNDATION
2291 West Broadway
Missoula, MT 59802
800-225-5355

RUE ENTERPRISES
138 Millbrook Road
Blairstown, NJ 07825
908-362-6616

SAFARI CLUB
INTERNATIONAL
4800 West Gates Pass Road
Tucson, AZ 85745

SLEEPING INDIAN DESIGNS
P.O. Box 8517
Jackson, WY 83001
Catalog available: 307-739-9802

WHITETAIL WORLD MUSEUM
P.O. Box 40
Clarksville, AR 72830
501-754-8620

WIMBERLEY DESIGN
133 Bryarly Road
Winchester, VA 22603
703-665-2744

REFERENCES

Bauer, Erwin. *Deer in Their World.* Outdoor Life Books: New York. 1980.

Bauer, Erwin. *Horned and Antlered Game.* Outdoor Life Books: New York. 1986.

Bauer, Erwin. *Predators of North America.* Outdoor Life Books: New York. 1986.

Bauer, Erwin A., and Peggy Bauer. *Whitetails: Behavior, Ecology, and Conservation.* Voyageur Press: Stillwater, MN. 1993.

Bauer, Erwin, and Peggy Bauer. *Wildlife Adventures with a Camera.* Harry N. Abrams: New York. 1984.

Bauer, Erwin A., and Peggy Bauer. *Yellowstone.* Voyageur Press: Stillwater, MN. 1993.

Boone and Crockett Club. *Records of North American Big Game,* tenth edition. Falcon Press: Helena, MT. 1993.

Brown, Robert D., editor. *Antler Development in Cervidae.* Texas A & I University: Kingsville, TX. 1986.

Calef, George. *Caribou and the Barren Lands.* Firefly Books: Toronto, Ontario. 1981.

Dalrymple, Byron W. *North American Big Game Animals.* Outdoor Life Books: New York. 1978.

Goss, Richard. *Deer Antlers: Regeneration, Function & Evolution.* Academic Press: Orlando, FL. 1989.

Laycock, George. *Whitetail.* W. W. Norton: New York. 1966.

Madson, John, et. al. *Outdoor Life Deer Hunter's Encyclopedia.* Outdoor Life Books: New York. 1985.

Mech, L. David. *The Way of the Wolf.* Voyageur Press: Stillwater, MN. 1980.

Murie, Olaus. *The Elk of North America.* Stackpole Books: Harrisburg, PA. 1951.

Putman, Rory. *The Natural History of Deer.* Cornell University Press: Ithaca, NY. 1988.

Rocky Mountain Elk Foundation. *Majesty.* Falcon Press: Helena, MT. 1993.

Rogers, Robert. *Great Whitetails of North America.* Texas Hunting Services: Corpus Christi, TX. 1981.

Rue, Leonard Lee III. *The Deer of North America.* Outdoor Life-Crown: New York. 1978.

Safari Club International. *Record Book of Trophy Animals.* Greenhorn Publishing: Rocky Mountain House, Alta. 1982.

Thornberry, Russell. *Trophy Deer of Alberta.* Greenhorn Publishing: Rocky Mountain House, Alta. 1982.

Wegner, Rob. *Bibliography on Deer and Deer Hunting: A Comprehensive Annotated Compilation of Books in English Pertaining to Deer and Their Hunting.* Watkins Natural History Books: Dolgeville, NY. 1991.

Whitehead, G. Kenneth. *Deer of the World.* Viking Press: New York. 1972.

Whitehead, G. Kenneth. *The Whitehead Encyclopedia of Deer.* Voyageur Press: Stillwater, MN. 1993.

Wildlife Management Institute. *White-Tailed Deer Ecology and Management.* Stackpole Books: Harrisburg, PA. 1984.

Wildlife Management Institute. *Big Game of North America.* Stackpole Books: Harrisburg, PA. 1978.

INDEX

ABOUT THE BAUERS

Erwin and Peggy Bauer are busy, full-time photographers and writers of travel, adventure, and environmental subjects. Based in Paradise Valley, Montana, the Bauers have specialized in photographing wildlife worldwide for over forty years. Their images come from the Arctic to the Antarctic, Borneo to Brazil, Africa to India, and other remote places.

Erwin and Peggy Bauer may be the most frequently published wildlife photographers in the world today. The Bauers' recent magazine credits include *Natural History, Outdoor Life, Audubon, National Geo-*graphic, Smithsonian, Wildlife Conservation, National Wildlife* and *International Wildlife, Sierra, Safari, Chevron USA,* and *Nature Conservancy.* Their photographs annually illustrate the calendars of the Sierra Club, the Audubon Society, World Wildlife Fund, and others.

The Bauers have more than a dozen books currently in print including *Yellowstone* and *Whitetails,* both published by Voyageur Press. The couple has won awards for wildlife photography in national and international photographic competitions.